"We too REMEM

*Cover: Drawing of Wests Centre, artist unknown
(the drawing is signed 'DW 1985' but neither the author
nor the publisher have been able to identify the artist).*

Daff Noël was born, the seventh child in a family of ten children, at the beginning of the German Occupation of Jersey. Her first book 'Remember When...' was published in 1995, followed by the biography 'Barefoot To The Palace' in 1998. With 'We too Remember When...' she returns to faithfully record more of her fellow islanders vocal reminiscences in her own, over-the-garden wall, chatty style.

"We too REMEMBER WHEN…"

Daff Noël

SEAFLOWER BOOKS

Published in 1999 by
SEAFLOWER BOOKS
1 The Shambles
Bradford on Avon
Wiltshire   BA15 1JS

Design and typesetting by
Ex Libris Press

Printed and bound in Britain by
Cromwell Press, Trowbridge, Wiltshire

© Daff Noël 1999

ISBN 0 948578 47 5

List of Contributors

Rev. Geoffrey Baker
Sir Phillip Bailhache
Eileen Barette
John Blampied
Rosa Borny
Mary Connell
John Day
Kathleen Day
Iris De La Mare
Jill De Sousa
Bob Gallichan
Leo Harris
Madge Hayes
Myra Hunt
Irene Hurley
John Layzell
Eileen Lees
Constable Bob Le Brocq
Peter Le Masurier
Doris Le Mercier
Lorraine Le Rossignol

Les Le Ruez
Jurat Mazel Le Ruez
Eva Le Sueur
Henry Letto
Joan Letto
Wenda McKee
Jurat Barbara Myles
Iain Nutter
Joyce Pallot
Alicia Priddy
Jill Sear
Arthur Swain
Peggy Swain
Gillian Thomas
Pat Tourtel
Senator Frank Walker
Stephanie Webb
Lady Anne Wilkes
Pat Williams
Kay Wills

Acknowledgements

Collating reminiscences for this second edition has been as much a joy as the first time around and I'd like to thank my lovely Jersey folk, wholeheartedly, for the many hours we've shared reminiscing, recording and chatting about our *temps passé*. I have been deeply touched by the warm welcomes and encouragement I've received.

It was also a great pleasure to receive the written contributions from Mary Connell, Jill De Sousa, Bob Gallichan, Leo Harris, Myra Hunt, Irene Hurley, John Layzell, Eileen Lees, Peter Le Masurier, Doris Le Mercier, Wenda McKee, Jurat Barbara Myles, Iain Nutter, Jill Sear, Gill Thomas and Pat Tourtel.

I would also like to record my thanks to the family of Mrs Rosa Borny for their agreement to the inclusion of her memories. I was delighted to record Rosa's 'petites memoires' as a gift to her six sons and their families on the occasion of her ninetieth birthday and we had discussed which ones we would include in this edition. Sadly Rosa passed away before this came about.

To all the people who looked out their old photographs – in some cases trusting me with precious albums – Thank you! And finally to my publisher, Roger Jones, and my two boys: bless you for your faith in me.

INTRODUCTION

Much has changed, even since my first book was published in 1995. Colomberie House, Sennett and Spears at Charing Cross, Orviss/Le Riches in Beresford Street, Le Poidevin in King Street, Brownes Fashion House, Foots in Union Street, The Old Soldier, Gaudins, the Aberfeldy Hotel (amongst others too numerous to mention), Chings Cigarette Factory/the Post Office Building on Mont Millais, Vienna Bakery and Grandfare at Georgetown, Barclays Bank in Halkett Place and St. Mary's Village Store are amongst much that has disappeared from our sight in the intervening years. With changes at the Old Fire Station; a disorientation game played on our familiarity with Voisins and the sea front of St. Helier changing beyond recognition, d'Hautrée School; Aquila Road Chapel; the Old Abbatoirs; the Pavilion; and who knows how many more, await a similar fate.

Yet, while we reluctantly come to terms with the inevitable, some of us remember when it was all so different. With very little effort we can recall bygone practises, extinct buildings, and people who once shared our lives. And so it has been while recording and collating this second edition of my fellow islanders' memories. Sharing the loss of so much that was familiar I have delighted in the mutual reminiscing and I am grateful to each one for the privilege.

I hope you will enjoy the experience too for, though I have spent many happy hours putting the work together, I maintain that this is not just my book but ours. Yours and mine, the contributors, you the reader who will be able to relate to our reminiscences, and future islanders – some not yet born. These are our memories of an island which was once so rich, not in financial terms as it is now seen, but in innocent character and gentle charm…Remember?

We too Remember When...

Remember when policemen directed the traffic in town? In the summer they wore white jackets and helmets.

ই২

Remember when vehicles and pedestrians gently jostled with one another throughout the main streets? Parking was never a problem.

ই২

Remember when our town boasted of local shops, who knew each of their clients and took pride in providing services, delivering goods 'on appro', altering garments as an accepted course, respectful of our custom?

ই২

Remember when fish was sold from barrows in the street, meat was weighed and sold around the country directly from the butchers' vans?

ই২

Remember when the ice-cream men rode their cold boxes before them on a pedal bike. 'Stop me and buy one!' ?

ই২

Remember when Hilgrove Street, or French Lane as it was affectionately known, became alive on Saturdays with members of our French population? The visits of 'Onion Johnnie', and the costumed Breton dancers with their beautiful, white, starched lace coiffes?

ই২

Do you remember the excitement, the glamour, the romance of the West Park Pavilion?

M̲y first real date, at the tender age of 15, took me to the 'Pav'. All the big events were usually held there. The impression you got as you mounted the front, semi-circular, concrete steps to the glass doors was one of grandeur. Stepping inside and past the ticket desk you were instantly confronted by a sea of red carpet which led you either to the cloakrooms and WCs on the left or up the grand circular staircase on the right, which stopped on a half landing before carrying you into the ballroom entrance, where you were usually greeted by two or three ladies waiting to take your ticket.

The whole ambience was one of excitement; the sheer size of the place, the height of the ceiling, the balconies, the waiters in white shirts with dicky bows; all added to the sense of elation and eagerness. As well as regular dances and shows I recall the thrill of entering several fancy dress competitions at 'the Pav' although I can't remember ever winning anything. Just to be at any of these places was a thrill, of course this could be because I shouldn't have been at any of them at all being, as I was, under-age!

Irene Hurley née Maiden, born 1946

Irene, on the left, at one of the 'Pav's' Fancy Dress nights.

We too Remember When...

*Do you remember when **John Layzell** was the Manager of the West Park Pavilion – the 'Pav' as it was affectionately called? I asked him to recall his time there and to explain how he came to be involved...*

To answer your question I have to take you back a little way as the chain of events is relevant. I returned to the island after the war in late 1945, having evacuated with my mother and brother in May 1940. My father unfortunately (having sent us on in advance) was unable to get away.

Most of the war years I spent in Weymouth helping to make torpedoes whilst serving my apprenticeship in engineering. It was during this time I attended some ballroom dancing classes given by a former Ballroom Dancing Champion who, by chance, also worked at Whitehead's Torpedo Works.

During those years, between bombing raids, I also continued to play football for the works team and, on occasion, for a Weymouth combination side in charity matches against various H.M. Service teams. My love of football came from the time I started as an eight year old at St. Marks School under the Headmaster Mr D'Authreau, and continued at La Motte Street School under the guidance of Mr A.B. Carter and Mr C. Miller both, no doubt, encouraged for the glory of the school by the Headmaster Mr Turpin. After school I joined First Tower Juniors.

I suppose it was natural that in 1945 I should pick up where I left off – I obtained a job as a refrigeration engineer with Jersey Refrigeration and signed on for my old football team First Tower United F.C., which was a member of the Marquis League, playing matches on Thursdays. However, at 21 years old, and feeling fit, I also signed on for the Sylvans which played in the Saturday League. Additionally I still loved dancing and the music of the great dance bands of the time, so I went dancing as many of us at that age did. Remember the Stadium, the Plaza at Wests, and of course the 'Pav' ? At that time in 1945/6 little did I know that I would eventually manage the 'West Park Pavilion Ltd' company.

In short it happened like this; I met my wife at a dance and we married in 1948. At that time the Brig-y-don Fancy Dress Ball was a huge social event at the Pav so, for that and other events her sister, who was a Ballroom Dancing Teacher, created 'The Babs and Reg Tanner Formation Dancing Team' to take part in these events. My wife and I together with other members of the family were co-opted into the team, which was very successful for some years.

Taking part in these activities some way gave me the confidence to apply for the post of Under-Manager when it was mentioned to me by Mr Edgar Becquet who, at that time 1954, was the President of First Tower United F.C. (small world!). I had an interview first of all with the Manager, 'Skipper' W.A. Mulley, and then with the board of the company under the Chairmanship of Mr James Belford, other members being Mr Le Cheminant, Mr Le Poidevin, Mr Beghin and Mr Maine, all proverbial, Jersey business men. I must have said something right for I was offered the job and I commenced there in November 1954 and stayed until I went to the Tourism Department in June 1966.

As you can imagine, working at the Pav was a completely different way of life, not only for me but for my wife and family. However, we managed, and I found Mr Mulley a good teacher. Of course older persons will remember him from before the war when the Pav, which was only built in 1931, was comparatively new. Much of the old values were still evident in 1954 and many of the staff had been there for a number of years.

Miss Moignard was the all-powerful receptionist, Mr Heaton the Head Barman, Mr Hilliker the Head Waiter (succeeded by Mr Jimmy Shaw), whilst Dick Geary and others gave him good support. Not forgetting the young Page Boys in uniforms, who showed patrons to their tables and helped to give the Pav that touch of class for which it was renowned. 'Sonny' Sloman was a resplendent figure in his Commissionaire's uniform and, holding all the cash and accounts together in the general office, was Miss Margie McKee, wearing her green visor. The resident electrician was Mr A. P. Hotton who also had a small electrical business at First Tower. Extras were called in, of course, depending on the type of function.

After a couple of years Mr Mulley indicated that he wished to take things easy so the Board agreed that he should remain as the Secretary to the company and I would become the Manager. This arrangement worked well until Mr Mulley retired and I became both Manager and Secretary.

At one time, about 1956, our Saturday Winter Night Dances were not doing so well so I decided to offer them to various clubs and associations such as the Jersey Young Farmers Club, the Telephones' Sports and Social Club and the Beeches Old Boys, to name but a few. The success of this move was to encourage more people to come back in mid-week, which improved our business considerably.

We too Remember When...

John Layzell (right), when he was Deputy Manager, with Frankie Vaughan and Manager Bill Mulley, 1958.

Bar Staff. From left to right: Bill Querée, Bill Langdon, Bob Mayne and Geoff Vowden.

I'm sure you'll agree the 'Pav' was the social centre of the island. Many people still remember the children's parties at Christmas time, with all the magic of Christmas around them and Sonny Sloman making a marvellous Father Christmas.

The various societies such as the Royal Commonwealth Society had their meetings there and over the years it was the venue for many conferences which Tourism had attracted to the island, all of which proved that the dear old Pav had many varied uses, not least of all in 1957 when it became the excellent venue for the lunch offered by the States to H.M. the Queen and Prince Philip during their royal visit. Here is a picture (see page 17) of the Queen and Prince Philip on the balcony, taken at lunch time, which we had processed and issued to all who attended the Ball in the evening. I remember the band that day came from the Army School Of Music at Kneller Hall. They played throughout luncheon in the 'Star Room' on the inside balcony, having sounded a wonderful fanfare at the entrance to the ballroom upon Her Majesty's arrival. Then their Dance Band section played that evening for dancing, regretfully H.M. and Prince Philip were not present.

One particular incident I remember concerned the licensing laws, so what's new I hear you say? Remember, in winter, one had to be on the premises by 10 p.m. after which no admission was allowed? On the occasions of Society Balls many patrons had evening dinner at the Grand Hotel and the party would hurry across the park to get in by 10 o'clock. Once, the Bailiff of the time arrived just after 10 o'clock and 'Skipper' Mulley, who happened to be in the foyer at the time, refused him entry. I imagine the conversation went like this:

Mr Mulley: "It's three minutes past ten sir."

Bailiff: "Yes, sorry I'm late."

Mr Mulley: "Well, the Bailiff says one can't come in after ten o'clock."

It was so funny. I can't imagine what the Bailiff replied but I suspect he joined his party.

I think, when the Pav re-opened after the war and a new dance floor of Canadian Maple had been laid, it made the best dance hall in Great Britain. Les Watson and his band were in residence and he continued until about 1958, when it became evident that a change was needed. By that time some changes had occurred on the Board. Mr Tim Voisin and Mr Cyril Tanguy had replaced some of the previous members and it was felt that we should look to London to provide a new band. Therefore we contacted an organisation called, Tele-Productions Ltd., which had been formed by Eric Robinson of 'Music For You' fame on the BBC and George Clouston who played in, amongst others, the George Mellecrino Orchestra before the war. They told a story of a number of professional musicians in London during 1939 volunteering for the Army, rather than waiting to be called up. They were drafted into the RASC and eventually persuaded the CO to let them form a dance band to play at various venues to raise money for tanks. The band became known as 'The Blue Rockets'.

After negotiations with Tele-Productions Ltd. we engaged a band led by Leon Mac, which came in 1958 and 1959 and was very popular with our patrons. In fact the band formed the basis of an augmented orchestra which played at the glittering ball given in honour of the visit of Princess Margaret, who looked radiant and stole people's hearts as she entered

We too Remember When...

the ballroom. What a night that was! The Princess danced with a number of selected partners, Eric Robinson conducted the orchestra and the cabaret included Jack Warner, Anne Shelton, Jules Ulmer, a very funny Frenchman, June Merlin, a lovely magician and the Television Toppers dancing team.

Above: The Royal Visit, 1957.
Left: John with Eve Boswell, 1959.

Leon Mac was followed by the 'Blue Rockets' the following year, led by Ronnie Rand who had been one of the original members of the Army 'Blue Rockets' (small world!). They stayed each summer until I left and Ronnie Rand took over as manager.

Of course the bands mentioned above only came for the summer season. It was necessary to engage local bands for winter functions, one of which was Cyril Holt's Band which provided some good dance music. Clearly there were many others. No doubt I'll be reminded of some when this is published!

Of the artists I can mention...Frankie Vaughan, who brought the house down at the Battle of Flowers Ball: Eve Boswell, at a Jersey Lions Ball; Tommy Trinder, who accompanied his favourite football team, Fulham Football Club, and Anna Neagle, who had graced the Battle Of Flowers that afternoon.

The Pav enjoyed a good run of success during my time but in 1966 I felt that ballroom dancing, which of course was our bread and butter business, was changing. Other forms of dancing such as jive etc. were being introduced and I did not think the two types sat well with the image I had of the Pav I started at in 1954.

Gone to a large extent were the 'Mixed Excuse-Me' dances, the Paul

Jones and, do you remember, the Spot Waltz? How we romantics loved it when the lights were dimmed and the spotlight shining on the mirror bowl reflected in a million pieces whilst you held the partner of your choice in your arms and for a brief few moments forgot all your cares, lost in the wonderful music and the magic of the dance.

Earlier you asked me for my best recollection of the 'Pav' and I said, "the night a very beautiful Princess Margaret attended!" However there is one other abiding memory, although it was in May 1947, well before I became manager.

It was May 1st and I became engaged, before flying off to Guernsey on an old D.H. Rapide to take part in the Muratti. My fiancée came later, on the special excursion, to see the match. Remember how full the boat used to be? The team stayed the night in Guernsey but I joined Ginty on the return excursion and that evening, where did we celebrate? Yes! That's right! The dear old Pav. We had a great party and fifty years later still have those happy memories.

I wish I could say the same for the Pav, which now looks a sorry sight. Hopefully it will one day be restored to its former glory.

I used to go out with my mates to The Pav, The Rainbow Room, The Plaza…great days!

Bob Le Brocq, Constable of St. Helier.

We went to the "Pav" on Fridays, for 'Teenage Nights', and how embarrassed we were when we weren't chosen to dance! In actual fact we were known as 'Wallflowers'. We could have died!

Mrs Jill De Sousa née Le Vaillant

I remember birthday parties at West Park Pavilion! At Christmas people would hold parties there at the same time, taking a table and having a party for one little child, then everyone would play games on the dance floor. It was all organized and you'd take home a little present.

Lady Anne Wilkes née Huelin

Above: Jill de Sousa, née Vaillant, on the far right, with friends enjoying one of the 'Teenage Nights.'

Below: Pupils of Miss Le Riche's School of Dancing enjoy their Christmas Party.
From left to right: Annette Perkins, Maureen Fisk, Maureen Le Quelenec, Wenda McKee, Guy Le Sueur and Graeme Gibaut.

Daff Noël

Wenda McKee recalls:

As a small child the Pavilion was such a special place to visit and one that was anticipated with a strong feeling of excitement and joy. Children's Christmas parties were very popular in the days of my early youth and to be invited to one, or to be fortunate enough to host one of these happenings, was a real treat. Best party dresses and shiny shoes, with the ribbons in our hair standing upright and to attention, were all part of the preparation for the event. Entering the Pavilion was awesome. It made me feel so grand. There was the smell of grown up drinks, smoke and ladies' perfume which mingled with the floor polish. Downstairs there was a place where we could leave our coats before turning to the right to climb the impressive, carpeted, staircase. There was a landing at the top of this flight and a settee and seats upon which people could rest and get a clear view through the interestingly shaped window across the park towards the Grand Hotel. The ballroom had a beautifully polished and shining floor that was so inviting to slide upon. However much the temptation was to race across it at top speed, then to see how far we could slide, this pastime was heavily frowned upon, as it was certainly not *de riguer* for young ladies to behave in such an unruly fashion!

There were tables and chairs arranged around the dance floor with the bandstand in the centre on the right. My father and the other musicians were there to provide the live music for these parties. An upper balcony with a wooden balustrade was reached after climbing more stairs and this offered a good overall view of the proceedings below.

These parties were extremely well organised with lots of dances and games like musical chairs and musical bumps – always a firm favourite! There were good prizes for the winners too! The high point, after the party food, was the arrival of Father Christmas with his sack of goodies. He made a grand entrance on his sleigh surrounded by suitably dressed helpers, some of whom had to be beefy enough to pull the hefty thing around the floor. Great care was taken to carefully wrap all the presents in a big box with brown paper and string and to write the name very clearly by the adult in charge of the child's group. Heaven forbid that the presents should get lost or mislaid! The parcel would be duly delivered and opened with great excitement! At the far end of the dance floor, on a small stage, there was always a grotto which we visited in orderly fashion, gasping in wonder at the glistening and colourful scene that

We too Remember When...

Left: Wenda posed in the large window that overlooked the Grand Hotel.

Right: Joint winner of the 'Hoola-Hoop' Competition

was depicted. I would dream about what it would be like on the way to the party. It was a magical experience and quite different each year.

One year there was an enormous stuffed black bear sitting upright on its haunches and towering over everything. I was terrified! I had never seen such a large or threatening animal and my imagination really took flight! In order to pacify me, and to allay nightmares, my father took me to visit this bear after the grotto had been dismantled following the party season. This poor hapless beast was kept in a dark passageway on the ground floor, which was only used by the staff and where broken tables and chairs were kept awaiting attention. I was still terrified! At last Dad managed to persuade me to poke the bear with my big toe, after he had demonstrated that it was really dead and perfectly safe to approach. Finally I summoned the courage to do this and raced away screaming my head off at my own bravery! After that whenever I had the opportunity I asked my father to take me to see the bear, for although I was still scared stiff it felt good to be brave occasionally!

It was at one of these parties that I made my stage debut. I was about four years-old and had been dancing for two years with Marjory Kaenal. We were fortunate enough to obtain some mauve net and my mother managed to find some matching satin and made me a very droopy tutu which I thought was wonderful and wore with enormous pride. My task was to perform a fetching little song and dance "I am the Fairy on the Top of the Christmas Tree" during the cabaret, which followed the party food.

I remember being very confident and waited patiently to be told when to walk on to start performing. All was well and I was perfectly happy knowing exactly where I should stand on the dance floor and wait for my music to start – that is until someone whipped the glasses off my face. That did it! I couldn't see a darn thing and all sense of direction went out of the window. However I wasn't easily fazed, made my entrance when summoned, took up position in the spotlight (I could see where that was!), performed my very best and left amidst the applause, feeling very special. Sadly this feeling was extremely short lived. Someone took me to one side and informed me that although I'd done very well indeed I'd faced the wrong way and performed the whole number sideways! After urgent discussion between all concerned, apart from myself, a very much older girl was instructed to dress up as a fairy and lead me on and point me in the direction for all further performances. Oh the shame and chagrin! My moment of glory had gone forever! However, some small consolation was at hand, for it was as the fairy in the floppy mauve tutu that I was allowed to accompany Father Christmas and his sleigh in the parade around the ballroom before delivering the presents. After some swift negotiations on my part I actually got to ride in the sleigh as well! This time there was nobody around to take away my glasses and I was able to enjoy what was going on!

I also remember that my family was always invited to join Kenneth Britton on the outside balcony at the Pav to view the motor racing. This event happened once a year and many big names came over especially with their brightly coloured cars for this event. I felt very special having such a privileged view with Uncle Kenneth whom I loved dearly. The popular band leader, Billy Cotton, was a racing enthusiast and one of the competitors. The noise of the engines was deafening and I can still smell the horrible exhaust emissions! The start was always exciting and noisy but the cars would soon disappear from view, racing towards First Tower only to reappear as they made the loop back towards town. It was hard to follow at times as the cars often became rather strung out and it was difficult to determine who was the leader.

The Pavilion is a special place for me, filled with so many happy memories. I enjoyed going there as much as an adult. I just pray that someone will finally realise that it is such an important place for us Jersey folk and restore it to its former glory so that it can continue to be used for special functions for many generations to come.

We too Remember When...

Do you remember those wonderful emporiums, founded in Jersey, that graced Queen Street? **Reverend Geoffrey Baker**, *son of Gorton Frederick Baker, of Frederick Baker & Son, recalls:*

Though I don't think I was very close to Dad, as time goes by I admire him more. He had a few good business ideas. He built up the business that his father, who had come to the island from Wiltshire, had started. Dad made it into a remarkably big business. People loved him. He was as good as gold, straight and honest and kind, very human. In those days places like Frederick Bakers gave their staff parties every year and everybody came and we all had a laugh together.

My two brothers, Peter and Arthur, just fell into the business because it was there. I don't think it was really their cup of tea. Poor old Arthur was bored stiff I should think. He loved the country life really, he had a lovely house and a big garden which he loved working in.

I remember when Dill and I were courting and we went to Sark for the day, we left our car outside the shop in Queen Street. We had no parking problems then!

At some stage in the proceedings Noel and Porters had nobody to carry on and our firm bought them out and Peter took over as manager. Neither of my brothers' sons wanted to go into the business so when they were offered a good price they were tempted and let it go. Noel and Porters went too. At that stage I was at our Guernsey branch. I had gone into the business when I came out of the Army.

Dad would turn in his grave if he saw how it had been sold and it was no more - but, perhaps he would understand? Who knows!'

I remember some of the shops which we had in King Street and Queen Street in those times... Frederick Baker's store, Noel and Porter's... and George D Lauren, which I remember as being a marvellous, old hardware store with a good toy department and all kinds of different things. It had a lovely old cast-iron staircase which used to go down into the lower part of the shop. All those stores have now gone.

Sir Phillip Bailhache

Daff Noël

I remember when I went to work at Laurens we only had an hour for lunch. My sister and I had a passion for playing draughts and we used to play that in our lunch hour. Of course we never had much to eat in that hour...I mean...what might we have...a tin of beans between us? Then the minutes seemed to be much longer than they are now, we seemed to manage to squeeze everything in. She'd be back at Boots for two o'clock and I'd be back at Laurens and we hadn't left work until one! When I was at the Bath Street shop I had to wait for whoever was going to take over from me so it was gone one then. We didn't have any tea breaks and Saturday we used to work right through until nine o'clock in the evening when you had half an hour for tea.

I used to meet a friend of mine who worked at Tregears. They had a little cafe above their shop in King Street and we used to have a cup of tea and perhaps a bun there, before haring back to work until nine o'clock. Later, when I ran the Bath Street shop it was nearly ten before I finished because the boss kept his car there. You see, he might have met someone to chat to on the way but I couldn't lock up until he got his car out!

Rosa Borny

Do you remember how Gaudins used to display the wedding cakes in their window and how we would look for the prominently displayed, iced initials of the couple concerned? How exciting it was if we knew them personally! Remember the man responsible for most of the special creations – George 'Bram' Le Riche?

Mr Henry 'Pat' Letto remembers:

My father had a jewellery shop in York Street which he'd started in 1913 and I was born, over the shop, three years later. We had a flat, well two storeys it was, over the shop. Living quarters on the first floor, and bedrooms on the second. We had to go downstairs through the yard at the back to the loo. There were two other cottages in the yard. We were there until 1929 when that building was pulled down and Dad bought the house in St. Clements Gardens and we moved down there. He had to vacate the shop, of course, so for a time, well nearly a year, he went into a little shop in Old Street, just to keep the business going.

We too Remember When...

When the premises were built in Charing Cross Dad was offered the corner shop and went into that from new. We're still there! I had a brother, Maurice, who was a stockbroker and Deputy in the States. He died in 1984. My sister Kathleen (Richardson) works in the shop still.

It was generally easy working with my father. He was a very easy going man. There were times when we had our differences naturally but we got on very well really... I mean he taught me my trade. I realise sometimes that perhaps I should have gone away to learn the trade but I didn't, I stopped here.

I met my wife Joan in 1938. She worked for Maison Burton the hairdresser, in Charing Cross, which was a few yards away from our shop. We got engaged the following year and evacuated in 1940 with my brother. We made for London first and stayed with an aunt for a few weeks.

We got married in Bristol, in 1941. I'd joined the RAF as an instrument repairer. When I went in they asked me what trade I was in and when I replied 'watch-repairer', they said, "Well, there's no doubt what we're going to have you in for – instrument repairer!" So that was it.'

Joan Letto née Fisher: 'There was a lot of bombing in Bristol so I was glad when Pat was posted down to Pembrey in Wales and I moved down there.'

Pat: 'I got a living out pass so I was able to cycle home. Then I moved about a bit after that and eventually ended up at a Bomber Station in Driffield, Yorkshire. We were up there three years, weren't we Joan?'

Joan: 'Yes, that was after our son Colin had been born in Southampton. You came down to fetch us and take us back to the house you'd found. That was in July of 1942. We stayed there until the war finished. I came home to Jersey in the July of 1945 and you followed in the August.'

Pat: 'That's right! My first leave in Jersey. We lived with my parents until we could find a house and I stayed in the RAF until I was demobbed in the following February.

I went straight into the business. It was just getting back after the Occupation. Dad had kept it going, mainly on repairs, because he was a practical watch-maker and jeweller. That's what kept him going for there was very little stock in the shop. It took us about twelve to eighteen months to get back to normal. We've never really looked back, though like everyone else we've had our lean years. We enjoy a good local trade. Our son Colin left Victoria College in 1959 and joined the business and, since my retirement in 1985, has run the business ably assisted by his wife Christine, my sister Kathleen, and a very efficient staff.'

Joan: 'Where was I brought up? Close to the harbour at La Rocque, at Maison St. Ives. My family lived there from 1921 until, I think it was 1937, we moved into town. There were four of us. I had a sister and two brothers. One of my brothers was the manager of Gallichan the Jeweller, the other one lives away.'

Pat: 'What businesses do we remember?...Laurens the Photographer! They were two or three doors away from our shop in York Street. In the old days everybody used to go there for their photographs and I remember there used to be weddings nearly every day of the week, with more on Thursdays of course. Three or four wedding cars parked in York Street. Just imagine it! And they'd be parked there for three-quarters of an hour whilst the bride and groom, and the bridesmaids, and the parents, all went in to have their photographs taken. He did a lot of business.

Besides our shop, Laurens the Photographer and Maison Burton (the hairdresser where Joan worked), there was A.A. Le Rossignol the chemist. He was opposite us. He'd been there for many years. Next to him was Eastman the butcher, he was on the corner of Seale Street, then there was Cawley the baker, where Horseplay is now. We used to go there for our bread but if we wanted wonders, dough cakes or vraic buns we used to go around the corner to Lipscombe in Sand Street. They were marvellous for their vraic buns and dough cakes. Do you remember them? Marvellous taste. Things don't seem to have the same taste any more.

Hectors were there, in Dumaresq Street and of course we knew all the Foots. Le Cras Baltus, stationers, stood where the open space is now and then next door to them was Burtons the hairdresser and next door again was Radio Electric, Kane's Radio Electric. Do you remember them? He sold radios and fixed them. He did quite a good business there. Then further along was Dupré the grocer. There were two Dupré shops, one in Charing Cross and one in York Street, however next door to the branch in Charing Cross was Bichards, the grocers. Cummings the butcher was next door again. He was the Constable of St. Helier. Next door to Cawleys was a little tobacconist shop run by Mr and Mrs Roberts, that was where the Steak House is now.'

Joan: 'There were lots of little shops in the area, and around Dumaresq Street, Hue Street. On the corner of Dumaresq Street and Hue Street there was a baker, Treyane's, who had his bakehouse behind that. He used to do the baking and his sisters used to run the shop.

We used to have the barrel organs around. There was one, a man and his wife, I believe they were Italian, used to live in Castle Street. He went around, with his barrel organ, selling paper windmills.'

Pat: 'What do I miss most?... Being able to walk up King Street, through town, and being able to say 'hello' to people! In the old days you knew everybody as you walked up town. Even in the summer with the visitors, there would be a lot of Jersey people about. Today you walk through and quite often you don't see anyone you know, well, not to the extent of the old days. There's not the same atmosphere in town at all.'

Joan: 'We say we don't see people but I think a lot of it is because local people don't come into town any more. They can't park very well and there's 'out of town' shopping. You see a lot more people in the winter. The town is not as welcoming as it was, there's no atmosphere and you miss the Jersey shops. There's so few of them.'

❧

Our town has altered so much now that I can't say "you turn left at so and so" because they're not there any more! Southwood and Mckenzie was run by three old ladies who became great friends of my family...Luces with its Eau de Cologne fountain. There used to be an Eau de Cologne lane in town but I can't remember exactly where it was- Noel and Porters, Frederick Baker, Lauren, De Gruchy and Voisin, Brownes...several libraries...the Penny Savings Bank. The town was quaint then, with its large variety of Jersey shops. It's such a shame...I don't think it's improved.

My parents, Mr and Mrs Towe, bought a shop at number 63, King Street called 'Au Paradis Des Touristes' and we (I had a sister and brother) lived in the flat above. Later my father built a house up Westmount called Hillcrest and we all moved to live up there. It was a large, very nice house overlooking the bay.

Though my family enjoyed the use of a huge garden with over a thousand fruit trees, Westmount became my playground and I can remember careering down that steep hill on a go-cart!

Alicia Priddy born 1908

❧

One night Roy Thomas and I were sitting reminiscing and we realised that we remembered all the shops, on both sides of Queen Street, the whole way down to De Gruchy. We started with Klein the dairy on the corner of Snow Hill, Orviss's Fish Shop next to Boots, then there was the hat shop belonging to Bakers, then Bakers, Laurens, Amys, Burtons, Woolworths, Noel and Porters (which took up a lot), Tylers Boots Shop. I can remember Dick's Shoe shop, Wilkins the paper shop on the corner of Vine Street opposite Woolworths. Hettich, Pearce and Assinders further up, can't you?

Most of the newsagents at that time were shabby, dark little shops except for the likes of Filleul and Queen, and Brookes. Do you remember Brookes at the bottom of King Street?

Kay Wills née Blampied

❧

Do you remember De La Mare's shop in Colomberie? During the Occupation I was asked to do some sewing for them. I knew somebody who was working there and he said to me,

"You do such a lot of sewing, maybe you could do some for us."

"Well," I said, "I'm not professional."

The next thing I knew I was presented with this beautiful linen sheet, which was a sin to cut up, to make a pair of pyjamas for an elderly gentleman who must have been pretty robust because he wanted everything cut on the bias!

Rosa Borny

❧

My most striking memory of our early days here was the fact that the baker called three times a week, an order to the grocer by phone was often fulfilled within the hour, and Mr Stone the chemist would deliver every day, as long as he was contacted before 2 p.m.! Service such as that was available on the mainland before the war, but never thereafter and I was quite overwhelmed.

Jurat Barbara Myles

❧

We too Remember When...

Before it was pulled down to widen the road in 1929 Le Caudey's had their bakers and general grocery shop on the corner of York Street and they had their treacle barrel in the shop. It had a guillotine at the mouth and you took your jug or bowl and they lifted the guillotine to allow the treacle to flow freely. Then when your jug or bowl was filled up they lowered the guillotine again. Underneath the barrel was a little bowl to catch the drips. I remember that.

You used to be able to buy potatoes in cabots, not pounds or kilos as we do now. It was a tapered wooden measure, wider at the bottom than the top, it was, with brass bands around it. They would put potatoes in and when it was full then that was your cabot. If you had a lot of big potatoes you wouldn't get near your value but if they gave you small potatoes then you got more for your cabot.

Pat Letto

Do you remember when all the butchers used to hang the poultry outside their shops at Christmas? There have been so many changes in town. Remember when the Fish Market was where the Telephone Exchange (Oh! It's Telecoms now isn't it?) is in Minden Street. Those people would come with their weekly catch of fish and you used to see the old ladies sitting behind their stalls, selling all the butter they'd made. Round pats of butter. They'd be there on a Saturday morning and they'd have come with their few apples and fresh vegetables. And there were the fishmongers who sold from their handcarts around the streets too. Do you remember all that? We used to have one young man who had his own fishing boat, who used to come to our house every Friday night. I remember once he came when I happened to be having a dinner party and I said to my guests, "Do you want to have some fish?" and he came in and sold out all his catch. There was fish all over the place! Oh! The smell!

Kay Wills

Daff Noël

*Do you recall Beuzevals, the popular toy shop which stood opposite De Gruchy in King Street, and how the proprietor, **Madge Hayes**, gave 'healing' behind the counter, even while the shop was crowded with customers? Madge reminisces...*

My husband had started up the King Street shop, Beuzevals, in the 1920's and when I eventually gave up nursing I went to work in the shop full time. It was a very popular little business. We sold cigarettes, tobacco, perfume and toys. The big toy department was at the back of the shop, which looked onto Broad Street. We had toys from all over the world. Customers would have a Christmas Club where they would pay in money, so much a week, to buy special toys for their children. I saw families grow up and return to buy for their own little ones. I still have

Madge, second from left, holding little David, prepares for the Christmas rush with family and friends.

one of the baby dolls from the shop. We always had a very good selection. My husband and I managed the business between us.

My husband Bert died in 1958 and I carried on with the shop. All the local people used to come in at some time or another. I knew them all. When I retired I continued to live above the shop but David ran it for me. I was still healing people. Locals from all walks of life used to come and I would lead them to a stool behind the counter and give them healing. I even had a doctor that used to come. I'd be serving with one hand and healing with the other!

I've been healing since the time I was nineteen. I had a little boy on the ward that couldn't wee-wee and he said,

"Nurse, could you put your hand on my tummy to make me wee-wee?"

"Oh!" I said, "I can't do that, I don't do healing." I didn't then.

He said, "I beg of you."

So I laid him down and put my hand on his tummy and I said, "Dear Lord, would you help him to wee-wee so he doesn't have to have an operation."

He squirted all over me and all over the bed. Everything was soaked. He didn't have to have the operation. That was the start of my healing. I've been healing ever since. People are still coming.

The Beuzeval stall at the Trades Fair, Springfield.

> Remember those innumerable, characteristic little shops that jostled with cottages to line the smaller streets of our town? **Lorraine Le Rossignol née Marett**, born 1940, recalls the years of her life spent behind the shop at 23, Hue Street...

We moved to 23, Hue Street from Rouge Bouillon in 1951 and I went on to spend 17 happy years there, until the States began their plan of demolishing the street. We lived above the shop at first, Aunts Lily and Laura Kent and I. These two elderly unmarried sisters had brought me and my sisters and brother up. Without them we would probably have grown up in the Home. As it is they believed in us all knowing how to do things like housework, washing and ironing, baking, sewing and darning. I hated sewing and darning, still do. Give me a roast dinner or cake to bake any day!

Michel's Handy Shop at 23 Hue Street.

The rooms above the shop were very small and reached by a flight of stairs behind the side door. On your first left as you went into the kitchen stood a big old wooden dresser past which was a tiny windowless room where I kept my guinea pig. The kitchen itself, once the gas cooker was installed, was just big enough to hold a table and four chairs. There was a black range which Nan (Aunty Lily) insisted on regularly blackening even though it was never used and the shallow sink, with its wooden draining board and one cold tap, was in a little cupboard alongside the window. Through a door on the left were the stairs leading to the loft. It was just one big room but it didn't span the whole of the house... and you couldn't stand up in it!

Along the passage from the kitchen was a little box-room where I slept and the aunts slept in the larger room over the shop. Upstairs again were the attics. No bathroom.

The shop below sold everything from flowers, to sewing cotton, to paraffin, though it naturally didn't have a fridge. Fruit and veg (loose, nothing came wrapped or bagged in those days), tinned foods, rice, flour, sugar. Behind the shop was a little room, with again an unused ancient black grate and a gas ring on which a kettle could be boiled to make a cup of tea. The outside toilet had been boarded off from this room and was so small that you had to sit down to close the door, and even then your knees forced it shut! We all used this toilet, even when we only lived above and the shop was run by the Michels. We had to go through the outside yard to get to it.

The aunts took over the shop in 1953 and I had to help out after school, Saturdays and holidays, for which I was paid 2/-d a week. Aunty Laura had the business head, Nan managed the house. We were taught the value of money and every week I put a little in the Penny Savings Bank which was collected and accounted for by each class teacher at all the Elementary Schools. I went to Halkett Place Girls' School for all but my last year when the education changed to including Secondary Modern and Grammar. So I finished my schooling at St. Helier Secondary Modern. I enjoyed my school days and have many happy memories of the girls and teachers.

When Roy and I got married – he had grown up across the street at number 20 – the aunts gave up their attic bedroom to give us a sitting room and we made our bedroom in the little room under the eaves. As time went on we shared that tiny space with our three little daughters. Our bed, the bunk beds and cot, plus the wardrobe (with sliding doors) that Roy built to take our clothes, left us no room to move. No one would accept that today yet we didn't think anything of it. It was our first little home.

Daff Noël

Twenty and a half Beresford Street, McKee's Music Centre, was the only home that I knew as a child growing up in what was once a beautiful island. My parents and I lived in the flat above the shop and my earliest memories are ones of being surrounded by music. It was not the modern 'head banging' variety but classical, light classical and the equivalent of the modern music of the time which was decidedly more harmonious than that of this era!

Left: The shop at 20 1/2, Beresford Street decorated for the Coronation, 1953.

My grandfather, Adolphus William, was crippled with arthritis in his latter years which made playing any instrument impossible, so he spent a great deal of time in the shop. Grandfather was seldom seen behind the counter, as he preferred to sit on one of the chairs where he could look through the door and window at the island passing by! When he wasn't thus ensconced he would be found standing outside the shop door chatting to the people he knew.

Every Sunday morning my grandfather would come into the shop and go through the paperwork and then take me for a drive in his car. This was a special treat, for it was a great number of years before my family owned a car and, being the only passenger, I would be allowed to sit in the front seat. It was never a long drive for grandfather had a short concentration span and became easily bored. We would drive up Mount Bingham or along Victoria Avenue and he would tell me how the island

We too Remember When...

had changed and developed since the days of his youth. Oh, how I wish I could remember everything he said in those days of long ago!

Grandfather said that he could remember Victoria Avenue being a mass of sand dunes before it became developed into the major thoroughfare that it is today, and of the family connections with the Jersey Militia Band. I own the McKee ceremonial presentation batons to this day. However, all this valuable knowledge came my way long before tape recorders became readily available and now I wish that all this wonderful information could have been preserved.

My grandfather had a deep interest in my growth. In the shop there was a section on one of the green painted, papered, walls against which I stood on each birthday to be measured and the new mark was recorded and added to the growing collection! I was given a crisp ten shilling note on my birthdays, when funds permitted!

My source of great joy was 'helping' my beloved father, Roy, in his workshop which was situated way out behind the shop and across a tiny open yard. The smells in there captivated my childish imagination. There was the dust of the ages, which was added to by every piano action that came in to be stripped, mended and rebuilt. Then there was the sweet fresh sawdust smell from newly sawn wood to be expertly worked and shaped to patch and repair instruments. The glue was utterly foul! It was made from animal hooves and the tiny shiny, golden amber beads were kept in an old biscuit tin. When more glue was required Dad would put some of the sparkling solidified droplets into the double glue pot which lived in solitary splendour on a gas ring, and add more water to the lower pan. When it boiled the glue would melt down – and the smell was appalling! This glue would be painted on to the wood needing attention with a very old paintbrush, the hair of which was curved, soft and pliable, when the glue was hot. This brush lived in the pot and, when cold, solidified with the contents! I still have, and use, the 'G' clamps which were used to hold the glued pieces of wood together in those far distant days!

Lots of interesting bits and pieces of instruments lay carefully arranged on the workbench and shelves around the walls, awaiting attention. My father was brilliant at being able to patch, make good and restore, anything that came in to be repaired so that it was perfect and like new.

These were the days before plastic had been introduced and the shop was predominantly made of wood, including the floor, counter, and drawers reaching up to the ceiling in which the mountains of music were neatly stored. Every drawer was carefully labelled and music could be purchased in different keys to suit the range of every voice. There were other folders in which the volumes of classical composers were housed and a stand that displayed the present day popular modern music. Across the shop window was a wire to which further copies of this popular sheet music was clipped and held by the upper left corner. I remember that the shop was very colourful with the attractive covers of the music, the cards containing the plectrum, the brightly coloured drum kits and the beautiful sheen on the wooden instruments.

Roy and Beryl McKee at work in the shop.

Guitars, violins, trumpets, trombones and percussion instruments were displayed in the window, on stands or arranged on the shop walls. There was always a good selection of recorders for school children to purchase, or have given to them, as their first instrument and we had a small glass-fronted wooden cabinet on the right of the counter which held the Hohner harmonicas. These were tuned to different keys to suit the performer. Because of hygiene no one was allowed to blow these instruments until they were purchased. Therefore in order to demonstrate that they were in perfect working order, and without fault, we used a hand operated bellows with a slot upon which the mouth organ was placed and moved up and down to test all the notes. Christmas was the most popular time for selling harmonicas. We used to keep the shop open until very late on

We too Remember When...

Christmas Eve and the normally shy and reticent Breton farm workers, with their faces well scrubbed like shiny rosy apples, happily exuding garlic and beer – usually in equal quantities – would come into town to do their last minute shopping and mouth organs were a popular item!

Pianos were a prominent feature in the shop. The uprights were kept on the right against the wall and the grand pianos were on the left in the body of the shop. Musicians would visit and try them out, comparing the tone, and deciding between an upright or a grand piano. My favourite was a baby grand and I loved playing the Steinway, which we had in our lounge directly above the shop. However, practising was always somewhat fraught, for there was always an expert hovering within earshot and I became very intimidated. Finally I decided to concentrate on dancing lessons. At least that way I could not be compared to some brilliant member of the family nor be expected to maintain the family tradition.

There was an entire orchestra of McKee's on the island, but that was before my time. My father was introduced to the orchestra at an early age. I remember him telling me about this somewhat unique orchestra. He said that as soon as he was tall enough he was presented with his grandfather's double bass and told that he had precisely ten days in which to learn to play several tunes. He did it too! There was not an instrument that he couldn't play and he had an exquisite touch on the piano. In the school holidays I used to love going with my father when he went around the island tuning customers' pianos. I was perfectly happy sitting in the car reading a book but very often I was invited into the house and would watch and listen, captivated by my father's skill as he worked with the instrument. As a true musician, and following seven years of intensive training at Chappells in London, he relied totally on his perfect pitch and 'ear' whilst tuning. He would have been deeply offended if he had been offered one of the modern tuning devices! The best part for me however was when he had finished and played one of his own special chord exercises and arpeggios to ensure that the pitch and every note were in perfect condition. These covered every note in all the octaves and then he would launch into a piece of music of his choice making the instrument sing with joy.

When I was in my teens, my mother Beryl joined the business and with dedication, determination, and not a little skill, made McKee's Music Centre into a thriving concern until my parents decided to retire in 1975. When they sold the 104 year old family business it was the end of an era.

Wenda McKee

Daff Noël

John Day recalls:

My father first went to work for the Quenault family in 1918. The firm had started out in Kensington Place, then moved to New Street before going on to Bath Street. We used the workshop in the photograph opposite until 1970. The stone walls were absolutely black with soot because of the furnace. They talk about passive smoking but, when we did the tinning the air in the workshop was absolutely tinted blue, you'd see the stuff pouring out of the door! It was the salamoniac, well we called it 'Toddy', that we used to make the tin run on the copper. You see, as you put the toddy in it's burning off all the time, clouds and clouds!

Before the war Grandins moved out from where they were at Commercial Buildings and moved to 80, Bath Street, next door to our shop. We used to make copper pans for the hotels, there was a hell of a lot used in those days – there's still some used but not so much today. Anyway what we used to do, at the latter end of my time, we took them to the Gas Works and put them in their caustic soda. We'd leave them in the soda over night because it degreased them, but in my father's time they could use Grandin's forge. One day Dad forgot about this saucepan

We too Remember When...

and when he went to get it there was a big hole in the bottom. Mr Quenault said to my father, "Well John (he always called him John although his name was Henry) you'll have to think of something", so he put a copper patch on the hole. When my father took it to the customer he said, "Well, you see, your pan was a bit weak there so we've put a patch on." It was perfectly sound to use so he got away with it!

The two Quenault brothers (right) at work. H.P. Day. John's father is the young boy on the left.

We've got some cans that we made over the years. They used to be sold for £18 a dozen. There was one other firm, down Charing Cross somewhere, that made the milk cans. I can tell you who made the cans by the shape of it. I can tell Mr Quenault's work from my father's, and my father's from mine. We also used to repair the cans for the dairies, on a massive scale. Because so many of them were used they became quite battered. We continued until they introduced the milk bottles in 1952. The cans were easily identified because what Samsons used to do was import the two halves and put the two together. All the cans have the horizontal seams but ours, because they are made from six pieces, have the vertical seams as well. It's very difficult to do that actually. I have the first can my father made and another one that Mr Quenault made for my father to celebrate his being with the firm for twenty years. We took all our valuables to England in it when we evacuated! We kept it with us all through the war.

My father took over from Quenault at Christmas 1946. He'd actually started on his own before that doing repairs for George Gallichan and Peter Nerac. Do you remember Gallichan and Nerac? They used to go around the country with a van selling hardware and picking up items for repair. They had a van, an old Dodge. My father put a window in the side so that they could display the stock. He used to do all this work in his shed at home. It was very handy because George lived at the top of St. Saviour's Hill, he had the shop there, and my father lived close by in Langley Avenue. What it was, George's wife ran the shop but the two partners actually operated from the garage at the back. It was nice and handy for, with my father being only about six doors down the road, they were able to pop in all the stuff like saucepans and kettles or anything else that needed repairing. That helped my father build up a bit of capital and take over Quenaults.

I started work there in 1947, I was fifteen, and I went on to take over the firm in 1970. I got on pretty well with my father but, in fact, it really was better when I was the boss. He was very good to me I must say that. You see it's all relevant. When you get to a certain age and you've got certain experiences, you tend to stay with that and you're prevented from looking for new avenues. My father was getting tired, he'd got to sixty-five and the business was running down. Things were changing so much, it was difficult for him. He really worked well for me though. Ah, he was as good as gold, working mostly part-time, three days a week. But you've got to move with the times you see. That's how we made a success of the firm really, because we diversified and went into other things.

My very first memory was at the age of three when we lived in Devonshire Lane. The dust carts were horse-drawn and even from that age I remember feeding the horse sugar. The horse's name was Glory. I can even remember the name of the person who owned the two cottages, my aunt lived in the other one, where we lived. De la Perrelle it was.

After that we went to live at First Tower for a year, at De La Field. We lived there whilst my father had his house built in Langley Avenue. He had one of the first States Loans. That was in 1934.

I was an only child for 17 years until my sister Jayne came along. I was seven when the war started, it's funny what sticks in your memory,

We too Remember When...

but the war was declared on September 3rd 1939 and my birthday was on the 9th and because of all the panic I didn't have a birthday cake!

We evacuated on the Isle of Sark, which was attacked by enemy aircraft in Guernsey. This was the last boat out before the occupation but we were lucky on one count for many people, when they came back, found they'd lost virtually everything. I mean, I can recall going down with a friend to what was the Bouley Bay Hotel, and the only thing that was in the whole of that place was a giant painting of Adolph Hitler on the wall. It must have been about eight feet by six feet, a huge thing. No floors, no window frames. That painting was the only thing left. Everything else had been ripped out!

Anyway, as I said, we were lucky because Le Gallais were responsible for storing people's belongings (the States took over the States Loan houses and let them out). By some fluke this chap, Vic Le Roux at Le Gallais, who my father had done some work for, spotted my photograph amongst the things sent down there. So he made a particularly good job of putting all our furniture in one room and locking it! We had most of the stuff, not everything, when we got back. Vic Le Roux was the head carpenter at Le Gallais. Did you know they had a wood carpentering shop? That was where the fire broke out, later on, in 1953.

Obviously, with our shop being in Bath Street, a few yards from the fire, we were called out and I can remember we had this phone call in the middle of the night. I got my car out and as we were driving down St. Saviour's Hill there were these great lumps of lino falling down from the sky! I'll never forget that! The wind was very high that night. That was what got it all going.

But the worst fire for us was when Le Masurier's went up because that was right around the back of the shop. The funny thing that happened there was that, doing a lot of copper work, we used to get our metal sheets half a dozen at a time. At that time they were four foot by two foot and we used to keep them in the stockroom which was above the work-room. To get to it was via a very steep flight of steps, in fact you had to stand on the work-bench to reach the first step. We didn't use it too often so it was all right but the night of the fire - I've always said it must have been the adrenalin - I carried six sheets down in one go! If someone had said, at the time, 'here's five hundred pound can you do it?' I'd have said no. It was just the sheer power of the adrenalin!

The force of the fire blew all the windows out of the opposite shops, St. Helier Garages, all along there. Le Masuriers had a big cellar where they used to keep their rare wines and of course when the fire heated up the large barrels they just exploded. All the whisky...well it was just like setting alight to something containing petrol wasn't it?

We moved out of the Bath Street shop and building in 1970 and into the premises at 43, New Street. Do you know we're still using the machinery that the Quenault family bought second-hand in 1885? You couldn't buy it. It's completely irreplaceable.

It's been very much a family firm. Kathleen my wife was delivering paraffin and methylated spirit for us up until last Christmas and Jayne, my sister, helped with the accounts for a short time.'

> *John's wife, **Kathleen née Godel**, was born at Les Ormes, Coin Hatain, St. Lawrence ...*

'I started to help out when John took over the business and kept the deliveries going when it became impossible for John. We must have sold thousands and thousands of gallons of paraffin. Years ago I had my own van, the deliveries were so regular. Every Tuesday the suppliers would come and pump five hundred gallons into the tank at Bath Street and I'd have to empty it all into one and two gallon cans. Then I'd deliver it around the island. Even up to last year I was delivering to an old lady at La Moye and two ladies at Anne Port.'

John: 'The methylated spirit? The hotels use it for the flambés. There's a good volume of that sold I can tell you. It comes in 45 gallon drums and up until last year we were actually fetching it from Huelin Renouf. The paraffin we get from Shell. Years ago we used to get a thousand gallons a week! Funnily enough we were having a bit of a sort out in the garage and found all these funnels and measures. They were all dated by the Weights and Measures. They test them and then they stamp the year on them.

Yes, we really put our backs into it, the business. Even on days like Boxing Day I used to do a round and Kathleen would come out to meet me with her van at La Crete, take the empties, and we'd load the van up and off I'd go again.'

Kathleen: 'And New Years Day!...We never celebrated on New Year's Day

We too Remember When...

because we were always stock-taking.'

John: 'We always did the stock-taking on New Years Day, from my father's time, we were always down at the business on that day. It was always cold!...oh..even though we had the Valor stoves roaring away. Your hands were almost frozen to the counter sort of thing! Kathleen and I were two years engaged before we got married and going out for a year before that.'

Kathleen: 'I was working in the office at Eastmans, the butcher in Beresford Street, and the lady who worked with me said there were two dining room suites cut right down to £27.10s at G.D. Laurens sale. They were only around the corner so I bought a table, four chairs and sideboard for only £27.10s!'

John: 'We were married at the Presbyterian Church in Midvale Road in 1956.'

Kathleen: 'A white wedding, two bridesmaids. Jayne was one of them and the other was my niece Angela. They were eight years old.'

John: 'I think my wife's still got her wedding dress.'

Kathleen: 'It was ballerina length!'

John: 'We spent our honeymoon in Guernsey but had to spend the wedding night at the Welby, now Mermaid, because we missed the flight!'

John: 'When I took over I couldn't afford the shop as well so I just kept the workshop at the back. The passage was just wide enough for us to back our van in. However the advantage I had was the tremendous experience of the business, and with Kathleen helping me we made a real go of it.'

Daff Noël

My uncle, Ernie Collet, owned the shop that made the corner of Cheapside and my mother lived above the shop. I was born there after my father came back from serving in the First World War and later, when I was two years old, we moved to 19, St. Saviours Road. My grandfather had a house there you see.

My Dad worked at Orviss, on the left-hand side where they sold coffee and that. When the old ladies came in he made up a little drop for them to taste and, if they liked it, he'd weigh up the required amount in a brown paper bag, banging it on the counter to settle the contents before folding down the top. There was quite an art to that you know because you wouldn't want it spilling out into the lady's shopping bag! There'd be a man on the door too, to open it for the customers. Those were the old days.

I used to go in with my mother to see Dad and I'd be given a biscuit or something like that. The biscuits were sold from tins that lined the counter and they only sold whole ones, never broken ones, unless you wanted broken biscuits of course. They were wonderful times.

John Blampied *born 1921*

I remember going to Orviss... And watching the overhead pulleys, taking the money to the central desk? That was fascinating to a child!

Lady Anne Wilkes

I remember the errand boys on their pedal bikes made of sturdy black metal, with the matching frame on the front for their wicker basket, and the name of their employers emblazoned on the cross bar!

Daff Noël

We too Remember When...

> ***Joyce Pallot née Mauger*** *remembers working at the Lexicon Bookshop. It was at the bottom of King Street – remember?*

It was about 1960 that I went to work at the Lexicon bookshop. Part-time, of course, because by then I had a young family; besides, my husband wouldn't have wanted me to work more than part-time, husbands didn't then. You couldn't run a home with four children and work full time. It was a great help though. John wasn't earning a large wage at the garage and we were buying our home. We had one of the first States Loans at one and a half per cent, which seems a ridiculously low amount now, but in those days it was quite difficult making the repayments on my husband's low wage as a garage mechanic. My husband was very good at handling money though, extremely good.

I was at the Lexicon bookshop for sixteen years, part-time, as I said, because of my family commitments. So that was from 1960 until 1976, approximately. My boss then was Mr Fred Hodges. It was only one of their shops because they had a group, Jersey's branch was Head Office for Guernsey, the Isle Of Man and Accrington, but they gradually closed. Once Mr Hodges retired the Jersey and Guernsey branches were taken over, first by Guernsey Press and after that by W.H. Smith. The other members of staff were Mrs Kathleen Pallot, my cousin, who was Mr Hodges' secretary (she was also in charge of the staff), then there was John Asplet, Miss Pygas, Miss L. Gillet, Mrs Doris Du Feu, Mrs P. Hall, Miss Beryl Jameson and Doris Collier.

The shop was very long and narrow, with pillars. We didn't have modern neon lighting, we had electric lights with white shades all the way down the shop which we used to spring-clean and wash once a year! We weren't asked to do it. We did it because we took a pride in the shop. There was an entrance at the back, in Dumaresq Street. For a very short time customers came in that way.

Our library was only very small and it was right at the top of the shop. It was usually run by a junior. Because I was part-time I didn't have a department so I worked everywhere, which suited my personality for I would have been bored staying just at one counter. I never knew where I would be working when I arrived each morning. Mr Hodges used to say, "Would you go on there for a few minutes?" or, "Take over that department, will you, because so and so is ill or unable to come in to work."

I also replaced staff on holiday so I worked in the office and store room as well, and the library sometimes, and dressed the window because they didn't employ window dressers! I found dressing the windows quite difficult because they were an awkward shape and had to show something from every department. All these things were brought up to the front counter. It was so difficult to get everything in that it was a real jumble when it was finished. I didn't like being watched by the passers-by either!

My favourite was the book ordering department. That was lovely. We had these great big red catalogues from the Book Association, called *Books In Print*, from which information we placed private orders and also got books for the Public Library. When the books arrived we had to check them in and cover them with plastic and brown paper. That took quite lot of work. We had hard and paperback books. It was so lovely at Christmas unpacking and handling all these very expensive books. We treated them with so much care! I especially liked the children's books.

We also sold Children's Annuals and board games were popular, in fact we had quite a big Children's Department besides an Art Department, Stationery Department, the Pen Department – I didn't like that because it was fiddly, replacing nibs and biro refills! And then we went into Fancy Goods which we hadn't done before. We sold nice Limoges china and jewellery and all sorts of things. We also sold records, 'Music For Pleasure', so we were expected to know that side of the business as well. The counters all had their own tills, customers didn't pay at a central till as they do now in so many shops. As you can imagine there was a lot to learn.

I worked in the mornings, plus three nights a week when I looked after the shop and was in charge of the juniors. We opened, I think I remember rightly, from 7 to 9.30 p.m. when I had to lock up the shop and make sure all the lights were out. Then I had to go to the night safe at the bank in Library Place with the money, which I wouldn't do now!

I got paid 10s. an evening – for all that responsibility! For my morning work I got £3.10s, which went up to £3.15s, a week. Out of that I had to pay my bus fares of course. The wages were very low. We had a very good staff discount, which was nice for me when my children were small, and later when they were going to College, because I could order their books. That helped a lot!

At Christmas we had such a lot of different stock coming in, every department was competing for space. We used to improvise, cover cardboard boxes with crepe paper, go up to the stock room to see what we could use. It was quite exciting at Christmas. We decorated the shop and didn't seem to mind the extra work involved. We took orders for the printed, personalised, Christmas cards too. We had people who came in just for those and we really knew those who were coming in. If they didn't come, for some reason or other, we really missed them. Oh! I almost forgot to tell you that we also did Wedding Invitations, so we knew who was getting married and when! We took bookings for the Opera House pantomimes too.

I remember going to the Rainbow Room at the New Era, Georgetown, for the staff's Christmas dinner. I don't think we had it in the latter years.

After Christmas we had the stock-taking. That was monotonous. Everything had to be counted, every card, every single pencil, every rubber. We started off doing the counting whilst we were slack, then we closed for two whole Thursdays. It was boring and cold, because the shops weren't heated then as they are now.

There were accounts and we were expected to know the customers by name. If anyone important came through the door we had to tell Mr Hodges and he would come and serve them himself. He was always on hand, never missed anything that was going on, but we treated him with respect. We didn't have a uniform but we were expected to be tidy.

Working at the Lexicon was very tiring, it was such a long shop, but I so enjoyed the work and the company of my colleagues.

Do you remember the Marina Restaurant at L'Etacq? **Alicia Priddy** *and her husband Harry took it over in 1949...*

We had a regular clientèle. They came from all over the island. We could almost know what the clients would want before they asked. The lunches – soup, main course and a sweet – were about half a crown, with coffees about sixpence extra. Teas – tea, bread and butter, jam and cake – were about 1s.6d. We catered for lots of Sunday School treats too and stayed open until midnight or one in the morning for suppers and dinners. I used to get downstairs about eight o'clock in the morning to start clearing up. We opened whenever people came in. If a family knocked on the door about nine o'clock and asked for a cup of tea I'd

Daff Noël

Mr and Mrs Priddy and their sons on the veranda of the Marina Restaurant.

say, "Come in!"

When we first moved to L'Etacq there was just a small room, a sitting room, bedroom and a kitchen/bathroom at the back so we built the restaurant and had a nice flat upstairs built on as well because we had three boys and had to provide a family home. We had a veranda up there as well. It was quite luxurious at the time.

All the deliveries came out to us. I just phoned up the butcher, baker and milkman with the orders and they delivered every day. We had a baker up St. Ouen's and a corner shop, which we don't have now.

I went to the pictures quite a lot when I was a youngster. You could go to the Wests for 4d. To get in you had to queue up that long arcade with the box office on the left... remember? The Forum was dearer, 6d... I remember 'the gods' of the Opera House too. Wests Cinema...One of my favourites were 'The Three Stooges' but I used to like musicals as well and cowboy films, of course. We'd come out of the pictures acting them out.

Constable Bob Le Brocq

I used to take part in shows at the Wests. We even went to live at 15, Hilary Street, a house belonging to the people who owned the Wests. Under the cinema, down below, was a big gas machine, for the heating and lighting. You didn't know that did you? The flame was all blue. It was a special thing that generated the electricity. By this time I was working at Birds bakery, starting at five in the morning, but the rest of the time I was producing shows and revues. We'd have dancing and

We too Remember When...

Cover of a 1945 programme.

singing acts and I'd play the guitar. Mr Green, the owner said, "You do it. You know all the people. I'll leave it all to you!"

We put them on in the cinema. There was quite a very large stage. Down in the front there was the orchestra led by Joe Pigeon, on his trumpet. There were ten in the orchestra. Some of them wore dickey bows but not all. We were free to wear what we liked but we were always smart. The orchestra used to get paid fifteen pounds a week. In those days if you got £2 a week for your day job you were lucky so an extra pound or so was very welcome. Whoa! Yes! That was something! And in those days we could play what we liked too, but you can't do that now.

Daff Noël

The Musicians' Union brought in copyright. Their man came over from England. Joe was with me when he asked how much we were getting. When we told him he said, "You're mad. You're not allowed to take that!" he said. "You're special people. In the union we don't allow our members to play for such a pittance!"

He went to the owner and asked him how much he paid us and when he confirmed what we'd told him he said, "I can't allow that. I'm afraid from now on you're going to have to pay them £5 or £6 each!"

"£5 or £6 each?" he said, "They've never had that!"

"Well, I'm afraid if you don't pay it" he said, "they won't be able to go on."

John, first on right in back row of the Amateur Variety Band.

Well, the next night the owner came to us and said "I'm sorry boys, I can't afford you all. I'll have the piano and the drums and that's all."

We'd been quite happy with our pound or so but the union decreed it wasn't enough. So we were left with nothing.

John Blampied

50

We too Remember When...

Remember the Little Theatre in Providence Street? **Kay Wills, née Blampied**, *recalls:*

At the time my husband and I lived in my family home at Trinity and, with my having trained at drama, we joined a dramatic club. Well, I suppose it didn't altogether suit us, so we decided that the only thing to do was to start up on our own, which we did. We had seven people who had joined us at the time and I went to see, the then Constable, John Le Marquand, who happened to be a very good friend of my father.

I asked him, something like, could I have the use of the Parish Hall to put on a one act play? and his words to me were,

"Your father would not have approved of that. Take Springfield!"

I said, "But we haven't got the people to take Springfield."

He said, "It's no good starting in a Parish Hall, that'll get you nowhere. You must take Springfield."

David Perry, who was also a friend of my husband and very keen on drama too, joined me and we both decided that yes, we could do it. We'd get the people to take part because after the war folk were only too pleased to join. So we went to see Springfield, which was either £70 or £90 a week, I can't remember exactly, but it was a lot because we had no money and only seven people to start with. We had no scenery either. We realised that we couldn't just put on a show. It would have to be a case of us doing everything.

I decided that there was only one play to put on, and that was 'Peace In Our Time' by Noel Coward. But it had a cast of just over thirty! Well, we put a small advertisement in the paper and were inundated with replies! So now we had both our cast and Mallacy Quarry, where we could make our scenery. It became obvious that we would need people to pay something towards it all before we started so we decided to form a club. Then it was a case of what to call it and that was how The Island Players came about.

(When we were building the scenery in Mallacy Quarry the first thing we had to do on getting home was strip off as much as possible outside, rush upstairs – my mother lived with us and she'd have a bath running – and get straight into a bath because the place was riddled with fleas!)

With the scenery organized we three, Sydney Fox who was one of our big members at that time, David Perry, and I, went around from door to door selling tickets. 5s.9d was the top price, then 3s.4d and 2s.6d. Those were the prices! Then came the opening night and we played to capacity houses. We made enough money to cover the cost of our scenery and on top of all that we were able to give money to the British Legion.

Up to then all the rehearsals had been held at my home in Trinity but after this success we decided that we wanted to have a place so we got the Mission Hall in Pier Road. We continued to put on plays at Springfield but it was not the perfect venue because it was too big. So then we had the idea of having our own little theatre.

Chings cigarette factory, Providence Street.

We saw this place, at Chings Tobacco Factory in Providence Street, in 1954, and of course it was built floor over floor. They were big floors too. We decided to do all the initial work ourselves. By this time we had about thirty members and we made up our minds to strip it all. We used to go down early Sunday morning and spend all day there.

I went over to London and, having seen in *The Stage* that the New Gallery theatre in Regent Street was packing up, bought their chairs. I went to other theatres, clambering up into the lighting stores, and bought second-hand electrical equipment. And then we had all this fitted up. Croad, I think it was, did the building work.

Now we only had about seven pounds in the kitty so my husband, who worked at the Trustee Company, arranged for us to borrow the money. Everybody thought we were absolutely mad to have this huge overdraft over our heads but my mother and I backed it saying, "Well, if it's a flop we'll bear the brunt of it," but I had no intention of it being a flop!

Did you ever go to The Little Theatre? If you remember we had a circle, as well as stalls, dressing rooms on two levels and two bars. We had a private bar for when we entertained VIP's and on top of that we had the general bar. The Editor of *The Amateur Stage* came over and he said it was the finest little theatre in the British Isles!

The Clubroom, formerly the Mission Hall, in Pier Road.

I was the licensee and well, we cleared the overdraft completely. In the summer I got professional shows over. Shirley Bassey made her first appearance in Jersey with us, so did Dave Allen. Then we had Joseph Weingarten for the music. He came over twice. We did all these sort of things.

However my husband's business grew to such an extent that I couldn't devote as much time to him as I wanted. We entertained a lot, sometimes we had two or three dinner parties a week, so we decided we had to sell. We offered it to the States. A complete theatre, seating 375 people. It was offered to them for £12,000 at the time that next door, which adjoined the property going round the corner, was for sale for £6,000. That would have given them a bigger site for under twenty thousand, than they have today with the Arts Centre! We seated more than the Arts Centre and we had a stage with full theatre equipment yet the States would not touch it. They let that go, they let the Forum go, and the Playhouse go, because there were people in the States who had no knowledge of theatre at all.

We gave up The Little Theatre in 1965. The building went into a sort of Youth Club, but that wasn't successful. Do you know, the most difficult thing of all was to give up the licence. I went to see the then Bailiff's Secretary, Mr Cutland, and he said,

Above: The stage before and after.

Below: The auditorium before and after.

The cast of the Island Players in the Gala Night performance of 'Trespass'.

We too Remember When...

"We know what to do to give it, and to take it away when people do the wrong thing, but how to take it back from anybody...." That was the funniest thing.

Before we closed we bought the premises in Union Street and decided to turn it into a Theatre Club. We were the first club on the island to own our premises. Our little theatre seats a hundred people. It's still there and we, The Island Players, are doing very well indeed. We've got over three hundred members now, very supportive members who come to it all, and we own our premises outright, no overdraft, nothing. That's something to be proud of, you know!

Yes, I've worked very hard on it all throughout the years, still do.

Memories of Aquila Road Methodist Church:

In the late thirties and forties most of the children who attended the Sunday School at Aquila Road Methodist Church came from the area around the church and walked there.

My sister Margaret and I could tell how early or late we were by the people we saw leaving their homes for Sunday School! Living in Winchester Street we walked past St. Thomas's Church and turned into Windsor Road where F.J. Carter & Sons were Monumental Masons. Joan and Eric Le Cornu lived on the other side. At the bottom of the road, facing us in Great Union Road, was Gallichan's the Newsagents, and a little further along was Du Feu's the Baker, where Barbara Du Feu lived. We then turned into Poonah Road where Gwen and Doreen Evans lived and Mr Evans had a shoemaker's shop. Doreen and Daphne Vasselin lived opposite.

On the corner of Poonah Road and Pomona Road Mr and Mrs Pugsley kept a grocery shop and all the family came to Sunday School – I think there were eight children, starting with the twins Mervin and Geoffrey right down to little Brian.

In Pomona Road lived Roselle and Brian Le Breton and also the Moyses, Jean and Roy, and the Ferbraches and the Balcams. Along Aquila Road lived Clarenda and Pamela Turner, whose parents were caretakers at one time.

Opposite the Sunday School door lived the Devenishes, who were certainly the closest and had no excuse for being late!

My first memories of going to Sunday School were of being taken by my oldest cousin, Hubert Le Sueur, who took Margaret and me upstairs and made sure we were happily settled in the little round wooden chairs. I particularly enjoyed the singing. Miss Barbara Hutchings played the piano and her sister Mrs Peggy Tostevin was the Leader of the Primary. I still remember the words of some of the little songs we sang, 'Dainty Wee Daisy', 'Little Bird I Have Heard', 'A Little Green Bud On A Bright Spring Day,' and many others.

The highlight of the church year was the Sunday School Anniversary when we would be taught our 'pieces' by Mrs Lobb and our songs by Mr Lobb, who lived around the corner at 20, Journeaux Street. When their daughter Amy was older she used to play the accompaniment and we liked that – it made our singing seem more tuneful! For weeks before the Anniversary we would go to the Lobbs' home to practise where there would be a queue of others waiting their turn.

There are many people today, in all walks of life and beyond, who owe their confidence, their ability to speak well or to sing, to this dedicated couple who gave so freely of their time, making sure that the performances were as good as they could be. There was no making do with anything shoddy or second best. We were well taught.

In the week before the Anniversary Sunday we would have to go every day to practise and on the Friday, when the stage was erected, we had the excitement of rehearsing on The Stage – built by the faithful Mr Husband – which extended over the organ and choir stalls, up to the level of the gallery.

When we were little we came in with the teachers and were helped up to our places on the lower levels, but as we got bigger we climbed up ourselves and when we were 'Seniors' we entered by the top door from the School Room and sat on chairs at the highest level. How grown up we thought we were!

When we performed we had to climb down to the centre of the stage so that everyone could see us! How nervous we were and how anxious to do well! The church was usually full with chairs placed in the aisles for all three sessions: the morning, when the Juniors performed, then the afternoon, which was taken up by the Primary. There was much 'ooo-ing and ah-h-ing' as the littlest ones hesitated and had to be prompted, or dissolved into tears, or by some miracle remembered the words and spoke up loudly and clearly, giving the parents the impression that they had given birth to an infant prodigy. The evening saw the climax in a

We too Remember When...

Demonstration, often written by Mr Stanley Picot, in which the Seniors portrayed a theme in words and music. This was sometimes repeated on the Monday evening, or there would be a selection of the best performances from the Sunday, before the prizes were distributed.

We all had new clothes and during the Occupation years our mother made us dresses from curtain material and one year she exchanged some of the precious tea she had been saving for a length of material to make us dresses.

Something else I remember was that all the hymns chosen for the Anniversary services were printed on special sheets. We had been practising them for weeks beforehand so that they were well known and well sung. I was quite taken aback to overhear one teacher say to another that she was fed up with a certain hymn, having sung it so many times! I thought she was so disloyal!

On ordinary Sundays, in the evenings, we would go with our parents to church and sit in the front row upstairs over the clock. I remember hearing the clock ticking during the sermon and Mr Hutchings sitting in the corner in a special closed-in box for the steward. He would come out when it was time for the collection. The Minister seemed a long way off in a special box of his own, and I wondered whether he was half way to heaven, or as I learned later, six feet from contradiction!

It all seemed rather remote to me as a child but it was a way of life and we wouldn't have dreamed of questioning it. I think we were more respectful and, although it was more formal, it gave us good grounding in the Christian faith. As we grew older, and became members of the church, our faith began to mean something to us and we found an affinity with those who had stayed with us.

Pat Tourtel née Pattimore

If Aquila Road Sunday School could talk – what wonderful tales it could tell! My childhood memories are many, always happy, and usually always singing! My earliest memory, though, is of my first Sunday School Anniversary when I was two and being taught a poem by Mrs Lobb about a robin - and having to turn to the right and point out of the church window. Not being able to remember the poem I am not sure why I had to point, but as in most of the wonderful poems Mrs Lobb taught me over the years, actions were usually required!

Singing, of course, played a very big part of belonging to Aquila. Our

Sunday School Choir was the finest in the island and we were very proud of that fact! With Arthur Lobb conducting, Amy Lobb (Luce) playing the piano, we practised on a Friday evening and twice on Sundays! Although I used to sing with Amy every lunchtime as well! I remember that sometimes on a Friday evening my next door neighbour, Pamela Baudains, and I didn't feel like going to choir so we used to hide in the passage beside Pam's house. Mrs Lobb, who was up to our tricks, used to come and find us and take us by our ears around the corner to the choir practise!

Happy - happy days - with loads of friends - Youth Club - concerts - Sunday school treats - 'bring-and-buy' sales - quizzes - and more concerts! - Christmas Parties - walks on Sundays - choir practises - the Eisteddfod - and even more concerts!

Yes - happy - happy days indeed.

Jill Sear née Ferbrache

A Sunday School Anniversary: I am greatly indebted to Jill for the inclusion of this photograph. There are so many of my childhood friends in this picture that as I look at it I am immediately transported back to those years. Pat is the lady at the front in the floral dress, on her left – in front of the boy in the suit, Michael Blampied – is my young sister Angela. Jill is the long-haired little girl three away on Michael's left. I am the girl just above Michael's left shoulder. My sister Daryl is also in the photograph as is my little brother Gordon who is sitting down on the far right front of the stage. I am looking in his direction so the photograph was probably taken at the time he was nodding off to sleep. I remember that a short

We too Remember When...

while later his inert little body had to be handed over the rows of the congregation until it reached my mother who was sitting towards the back.

The Lobb family, Mr and Mrs Lobb, John, Arthur and Amy devoted their lives to us children, teaching us, involving us in concerts and entering us in the Eisteddfod. They were part of a special breed of talented islanders who gave their time for the pure enjoyment of it. Not one penny payment was expected in return for the innumerable lessons they gave.

My recollections of Sundays are dominated by the Chapel, first with Royal Crescent and then because of our move to town, with Aquila Road Primitive Methodist Church. At first we attended Sunday School twice a day, mornings and afternoons, with a break in the summer when it dropped back to mornings only. In those early days we sat at tables on little semi- circular backed chairs and listened to simple Bible stories, knowing that when the teacher had finished we'd be able to colour in pictures of that story on leaflets which we could take home to read again.

When we were a little older we joined the grown-ups for the remainder of the service, taking up the pews on the balcony. The sermons, naturally directed at the adults, were very boring for us children. I remember my friends and I would try to sit in the front row. From there we could not only count how many grown-ups were nodding off, or see who had a new hat, but we could play the 'confetti' game, tearing off tiny corners of the leaflets and letting them drop discreetly onto the heads of the congregation directly below!

I cannot imagine what my early life would have been like without the dogma, the generosity, the bias, the fun and the romance, of the years I attended Aquila Road Chapel.

Daff Noël

My parents were Methodists and attended Aquila Road, where I was dragged to attend the services every Sunday. I must admit I did not enjoy it. There were some lovely Ministers but it was very boring for a child.

Senator Frank Walker

I used to go to Aquila Road Youth Club when George and Pam Marett ran it. I wasn't too bad at table tennis though I didn't go in for competitions. I remember Michael Tourtel and Pat Pattimore who became his wife and Brian Le Breton. A group of us, including Ruth Pallot, Brian's first wife, would go cycling on Sunday afternoons.

Pat Williams née Le Masurier

Daff Noël

I've always had a great faith. When I first came to Jersey I went to the Presbyterian Church then I went to Great Union Road where I was a Sunday School Teacher. I used to help Gordon Coombs when he produced the Pantomimes there. We had a wonderful time. Later on Great Union Road amalgamated with Aquila Road so I started to go there.

Madge Hayes

My children, Paula and Gill, used to go to Madge Beuzeval's Sunday School, in Great Union Road. Her husband was a lay preacher there. They put on pantomimes and concerts. Do you remember? There were loads of things, including prize giving. I don't know if the children get prizes now, do they?

Iris De La Mare née Morris

A Pantomime cast of 'Aladdin'. Gill (De La Mare) is the little girl kneeling on the far right.

We too Remember When...

***Joyce Pallot née Mauger** was born at Rose Hill, Sion, in 1923...*

I always went to Sunday School, even from a very early age. My aunt, Florence Mauger, was in charge of the Sunday School at Augrés Chapel and we attended twice on Sundays, morning and evening, walking all the way from Sion. Later my Dad had a motor bike and side-car so we had a ride with him and, much later again when he had a car, but most of the time we walked. We always had nice Sunday best clothes. My aunt wouldn't cycle on a Sunday because she had her best clothes on! She'd cycle in the week but not on Sundays! Life revolved around Chapel. We met our partners at Chapel, or rather after Chapel. They were waiting outside!

I started school with Miss Virginia Coutanche whose school was above the Post Office at Sion, opposite the cemetery where the Spar shop is now. The Post Office was run by one sister, the school by another, and their brother did the baking! I was there until I was about ten and then I moved to Vauxhall Private School at 62, New Street. One of the teachers, Miss Una Godeaux, was a friend of my mother's so that was why she put me there.

The school was on the side of the old Playhouse Theatre. We went in by the back entrance, a little covered passageway, in Le Geyt Street. There were three rooms, two teachers and a pupil teacher who had been one of the senior girls and who had left. She looked after the beginners.

I was quite happy there. We wore very smart, maroon gym dresses and white blouses, a maroon and navy tie, with a maroon waist girdle. We were mostly girls though we did have a few boys, usually for only a brief time. We learnt the three 'R's' and our parents had to pay extra for music, singing, dancing and gym. Yes, I did the dumbbells and clubs! We went across to the Wellington Hall, in Union Street, for all that. We learnt singing with Mr Allen. Mr and Mrs Allen taught music in a few schools, as did Miss Enid Le Feuvre with her elocution lessons. She was very good. She taught us to speak out. Miss Le Feuvre was at Augrés chapel as well.

I went into town on the bus, there were quite a few bus companies then. I must have got off the bus in David Place because I can remember, at first, we used to walk up Vauxhall Street to catch the bus back home. Later on they must have changed the route because we started catching it in the Parade. I left school at fourteen. I could have stayed on, but I wanted to leave. By this time, because there was one senior class and

Daff Noël

one teacher, we were more or less doing the same work as the younger ones.

I went to work in Hill Street, as a junior in an accountant's office, Read, Son and Cocke. I found it very difficult at first. I started off doing the messages and sticking on stamps. I was there all through the war. It was quite a big firm but the staff all evacuated, except one of the senior staff. We were then only two. By that time I was doing the typing and lots of other work. My boss, Mr Ian Henderson, went over to England so after the Liberation I was the only one running the office while I was waiting for the others to come back.

When I arrived in the morning I would light the open coal fire, when we had fuel of course, and as there wasn't much to do my friends used to just pop in for a chat. I was very junior and life was very easy. I used to leave a little note on the door sometimes, "Back in ten minutes!" and wander around the shops. Frederick Baker was my favourite shop. That was a lovely shop, it had so many departments. I was there, at Read, Son and Cocke, for about eight years.

During the Occupation I spent most of my wages on having clothes altered, clothes that had been passed on by relatives. We had a dressmaker at Sion, Mrs A. Bochat, who used to make coats from blankets. We used to have our clothes made out of all kinds of materials.

I met my husband, John, before the war, at Sion Chapel. He also worked at the garage next door to my home. I was still at school then. We were good friends from the start. Then he evacuated and joined the Army, and I didn't see him for five and a half years. We could only send Red-Cross messages to each other.

John came on leave twice after the Liberation and when he was demobbed a year later we were married within a fortnight. Looking back it was quite amazing because all we had exchanged in the time we were apart were the few words in the Red Cross letters.

We only had one holiday away whilst the children were growing up but we used to plan our holidays here in Jersey. My husband only had a week's holiday, seems unbelievable nowadays, doesn't it, when people have five or six weeks. Still I used to plan that week very, very carefully. We always went somewhere we'd never been before. We'd go out every day, taking picnics. Wonderful family picnics. They were lovely times. My husband and I were married for thirty-four years before he died.

We too Remember When...

Eva Le Sueur née Le Rossignol *remembers...*

I've got one brother, he's two years younger, and we grew up at 17 Duhamel Place. It was one of two houses, numbers 15 and 17 were merged into one, that belonged to Mr Duret Aubin. Mr Le Sueur (no relation), who was the States Veterinary Surgeon, had his surgery at number 15. There were big stables at the back with cows and horses. My father was his assistant and he used to make up all the powders and medicines for the sick animals. Dad was always out with the vet. Mr Le Sueur had one of the first motor cars in Jersey, an old Renault, and a horse and trap. We had animals all around us for Mum and Dad were also caretakers. It was very interesting.

I went to school at Halkett Place Girls', which was only round the corner, and as I grew up I used to help in the surgery on a Saturday, taking the farmers money and giving them their receipts.

The Headteacher at Halkett Place was Miss Lucy Daniel. She was very good. I was there the first year they brought in scholarships for the Girls' College, and I passed, but my mother said I was too valuable for her at home. She wasn't well, so I couldn't go. I would have loved to have gone to the College because I was very interested in my school work. The same year I won the prize for General Knowledge given by the Diocese of Winchester and Miss Daniel had my certificate framed and hung up in the school. I would have liked to have kept it but Miss Daniel said, "Leave it there for the time being". I never did have it. I was at Halkett Place all of my school life. I was there of course during the First World War and I remember the Roll of Honour being put up on the wall at the back of the building, in Don Street.

When the States Vet retired, and went to live out at Samarès, the house was put back into two. The other house, number 15, was let to a music teacher, Miss Libby. She was a lovely lady and very clever. She used to organize these sing songs with Mr Thomas Marguerie, Lyndon Marguerie, and Beryl Jordan. Beryl was a friend of mine. They were all very musical. I was learning piano at the time. Mum and Dad bought me a lovely piano and we had it in the back room. I used to practice all the time, all the latest. If any new songs came out (you could buy sheet music at Woolworth for 6d), I would try and play them.

The people on the other side to us, the Maugers, left and the Le Sueurs moved in. One night I was practicing when I heard a voice say, "Is that all you can play?"

I looked outside and saw this young man, Arthur. I didn't know it then but he was to become my husband. I said,

"What do you mean? What's wrong with that?"

And he said, "Haven't you got anything decent?" I remember that! "Haven't you got anything decent, to play?"

I said, "That's decent!"

His sister came out and she said, "Don't take any notice of him. Close your window and carry on."

So I closed the window and carried on.

A couple of nights after we had the same nonsense again, with him making comments, and this went on for a while. Then one night he said,

"Do you fancy coming down to the bathing pool tonight? They've got a little dance on and you'll hear some real music."

I said I didn't know but Mum said 'go on!' so off I went. I remember my dress, I'd kept it for something special. It was white and pale blue voile. I was only about eighteen. That's how we started. We used to go down the pool a lot after that, and Billy's Lido for coffee. Remember Billy's Lido?

The bathing pool was very popular, no wonder islanders want to keep it. It was lovely with all the lights. There are a lot of people like me who have lovely memories of the tea dances, and the swimming and diving there. When they were talking on Radio Jersey about whether they should save it I nearly rang up and begged 'please don't let it go!' I'm glad they're doing something with it. So many people like me have many happy memories of that place.

We courted a long time before we married. Well, I was working in Guernsey for a time you see, because the Post Office there was short-staffed and the overseer asked me if I would like to go across to help them out. They wanted two people he said. Well, I said, I would speak to my Mum and Dad about it – 'cos you had to in those days, not like now. The overseer said, "Go now. Leave your desk, and go now!" so I went and saw my Dad and he said, "What a good idea! It'll do you good. Not that I want to get rid of you, but it'll do you good."

So I went in to Mum. Oh! No! I wasn't to go! No fear!

But I did go. The other girl that came with me was Joyce Rattenbury. We shared a room together. She stayed a little longer than me but I stayed all the summer. I used to write home, you didn't phone in those days. But I loved it in Guernsey and there was a young man I liked. Oh! He was

We too Remember When...

nice! Joyce had a young man as well and the four of us would go for picnics on a Sunday. We had a lovely time, we really did. I lived right opposite Victor Hugo's house in Hauteville. It was called Old Holme. Lovely place. One day she came to me and said, "You've got a visitor. In the dining room." It was my Mum.

"Hello Mum!" I said. "You didn't tell me you were coming."

"No," she said, "because you're coming back with me that's why!"

"Oh! No!" I said. "I can't leave without a month's notice." After a bit of a talk I said, "I'll come back to Jersey, yes, but I've got to work my time. Why don't you stay for a few days and I'll take you around." Well she agreed to that but when she left she said, "Mind you come back now. I don't want you staying in Guernsey permanently!"

It was a different world to today. Young people were friends and the young men treated you with respect. You looked up to your parents too.

I was working in the Telegraph section at the Post Office. I had to train for it, putting the telegram into Morse code. In fact I still have the Morse books. I've kept them. The people who wanted to send a telegram would hand it in at the counter, then the assistant would send it up in the tube to us and we would change it into Morse. That was until the tele-printers came out. We had a line to St. Malo but, well, my French wasn't all that good and sometimes the words didn't come out right, and the chap over there used to swear at me in French! I was at the Post Office until the war.

My family stayed at Duhamel Place for a while, then Mum and Dad bought a house at Coastlands, Grève D'Azette. I got married from there, my brother did as well. When I came back from Guernsey I'd started going out with Arthur again and we were married in 1939. Then the war upset everything. We were all set to evacuate. Arthur's brother Ronnie had gone into the RAF, the other one had closed his shop and gone, but my Dad had said, "Germans or no Germans I'm not going. That's it!"

My mother and father-in-law were staying but the others hadn't said goodbye, so the day we were going my husband cycled up to their house. Well, my mother-in-law was very, very deaf and after calling out and searching for her he heard a noise coming from under the stairs.

It was his mother, crouched down.

"Come on out Mum!" he said.

"I thought I heard a plane," she said.

He had a job to get through to her, because she was so deaf, to tell her we were going.

"They've gone!" she said, "and they've left me notes because they couldn't say good-bye. You're not leaving me, are you? Ah! my love, you're not going, are you? You wouldn't leave me?"

He came back in tears. "What can I do?" he asked.

"Well," I said, "my father's sitting in his garage, refusing to go and I'm not going without him so…"

We stayed here. They were building a pretty little bungalow at the back of Coastlands and my husband and I asked if we could have it. We moved in 1941 and I stayed on alone, with my little doggie Holly, for ten years after he died.

I remember when the butcher and baker, Keith Baal, were on the corner of Green Road and it was known as 'Baal's Corner'. Mrs Houseman ran the shop on the other corner. She, and her husband, he was lovely too, sold everything. He was organist at St. Mark's Church. Lovely couple. Do you know we had everything we needed round about. The shops were really handy.

The first dinner dance I went to, it was with my husband, was at the Hotel de L'Europe. The dressmaker made me a beautiful dress in blue velvet and the singer sang the song. Now, whenever 'Blue Velvet' is played, the memories come rushing back. We went to the Pav too, often. I remember the Pav when it was the Tin Hut. They used to have skating there as well. My husband enjoyed skating. He was a great swimmer too. Anything with the sea he loved. He was a real live wire. He was a member of the Green Room Club and used to take part in their shows. He loved it. He worked for the JEC.

If I had to live my life again I wouldn't change anything. We were married for forty-one years before he died. And we have two lovely girls, really lovely. I'm so lucky.

We too Remember When...

Do you remember the age of the telegram?
Alicia Priddy, née Towe, *remembers it well...*

In the school holidays I worked for the Post Office and carried on working there when I left school finally. I had to know Morse code though I can't remember any of it now. In the potato season I worked in an upstairs room typing out telegrams which were transcribed into Morse code before they arrived at the machine in England, where they were translated into English again before being sent out. When they came to Jersey the procedure was reversed. The telegrams came in a tube, on a narrow strip of paper. I had to translate the Morse coded messages into English, write out the envelope and place them in a round tube. Then I put them in a hole in the floor, and pressed a button to send them down below to the sorting office, where they were put into areas before being given to the boys to deliver.

We had a small band of telegraph boys then who delivered around the island by bicycle. For two or three years in succession I was sent to Guernsey for the tomato season. I thoroughly enjoyed it, finding the people very nice.

I retired from working at the Post Office when I married my husband Harry in 1929 because by then I had the restaurant at Portelet to run.

Harry, my husband, was brought up in Devonshire Lane, my sister's husband was brought up in Cannon Street, and we all went to All Saints Church.

We knew Donald Labey, 'Uncle Labey' as we used to call him, do you remember him? He was very musical, used to play the organ at All Saints. In those days we used to have Whist Drives and dance evenings. Never just Whist Drives. We'd play whist until ten o'clock, then someone would play the piano and we'd dance until midnight. We used to go there every week in the winter and 'Uncle' Labey would play the piano whilst we danced. I think we made far more of our own amusement in those days. We all made our own fun. We had either lemonade or coffee to drink and everyone was always nicely behaved.

The churches benefited from these events because they used to run them and collect two shillings to half-a-crown, and after we paid the rent for the hall they kept the rest. The Church was the hub of life then.

In the Occupation we had the café, just above the holiday camp at Portelet, and of course the Germans took over the camp so I immediately closed. One day there was a bang on the door and when I opened it I found two German Officers standing there and they said,

"What is this place?"

I said, "It's a café."

"Are you open?"

I said, "No, I'm not open"

They asked, "Who lives here?"

I said, "I do, with my three small sons."

"Where is your man?"

I said, "I have no idea, he's in the British Army."

Oh well, he looked me up and down and then said,

"I advise you to open. Otherwise, I will have to billet German soldiers on you and that will not be nice."

I said, "No, it wouldn't."

So he said, "Go to whoever is necessary in town and get the permission you need to open."

So I did. I had quite a lot of local customers who used to come for lunch and that sort of thing because my father kept a lot of chickens. He also had a big garden and grew his own vegetables.

The Germans used to come in but they weren't allowed to have anything to eat, just tea or coffee. Luckily I had bought up plenty of tea at the beginning of the Occupation knowing that I'd need it and the coffee I made from parsnips, grating them, drying them and roasting them in the oven until they were a coffee colour. You used that to make your coffee. It was very nice, slightly sweet being parsnip. The Germans and locals used to drink that.

As I say I had quite a lot of people who used to come in for Sunday lunch and that sort of thing. Half-a-crown a head. Things went quite well. The Germans came of an evening but I used to turn them out at ten o'clock, or nine o'clock, whichever was the curfew. They'd sit and chat and play cards. They used it as a clubroom. They were very good really, for very often I'd find a loaf of bread, or something or other, left on one of the chairs for me, you know. To be perfectly honest they were better behaved than the British soldiers. They were gentlemen in comparison to some of those we had. The Germans were always showing me photographs of their wives and children. They were always very worried because I didn't get any letters from my husband, and didn't know what part of the world he was in. They used to play with the boys, and that sort of thing, and were always very polite to me.

We too Remember When...

There was petrol to start with, before it was rationed. My customers used to use their ration, or cycle, or come in a horse and cart. Actually I think in lots of ways we were lucky on the island because the Occupying forces behaved themselves.

I had my first café in 1929, when I got married. It was behind the Finistere Hotel at Ouaisné. Then my father bought the Medina at Portelet and built us a café in the garden. That's where I was during the Occupation. We took over the Marina at L'Etacq in 1949. I stayed there until 1963 when my son Dill took it over.

ે

It was in the autumn of 1947 when I was talking to the Potter twins, Austin and Charles (I knew Charles, or Mr Potter as I always called him, as before the Occupation I was at school with his step-daughter Roxana and used to visit their home, Old Cadet House, on Gorey Hill and stay for the weekend or an odd night). Well, in the course of conversation they told me about the pottery they had started in Gorey Village. The reason was not on account of their name but because their nephew, Austin Wood, had recently been demobbed from the Navy and was in need of a job. I told them I was too and was immediately offered one as 'odd job girl'.

So a few days later I got on my bike and cycled to the village. The pottery was not a large one, just a shed behind the main street. There were two floors and an office up a spiral staircase. At that time there were five men working there and ME! A Very Odd Job Girl!

The men were Austin Wood, the manager and designer who also did some throwing; Ivor Leaman, who had come over from Bernard Leech's studio in Devon as the chief thrower; a young man, whose name I am afraid I have forgotten, who was a scientist, and who mixed and made the colours to decorate the pots; an old man (at least he seemed old to me!) who had to beat and thump and slap the clay to get all the air out before it could be used and the fifth man, Donald, Charles Potter's stepson. He helped decorate the pots, I should say 'ashtrays' as in those early days that is all we made!

My main job was fettling or, as I used to call it, smoothing bottoms. This entailed removing the rough edges of the dried ashtrays before they were decorated and fired. I also had to stamp 'Jersey Pottery' on the bottom of each.

Another very important job I had was making the tea or, as in most cases, making the Oxo. Maybe we couldn't get milk and sugar, I don't know, but certainly it was Oxo cubes I put into the mugs before adding the boiling water from a kettle that I had heated on a paraffin stove which had to be pumped up to get it to light. I was always afraid it would explode!

After a short while our team began to grow. Another thrower came from Wales – Tony Griffiths. He took over the second wheel, letting Austin get on with designing other artefacts, and another girl from the village, Irene… well, I got her to pump the stone so that I could get on to putting the slip – the soft coloured clay – on to the pots before they were fired. I also did the glazing – dipping the pots into the transparent glaze, which made them really hard, water-tight and shiny.

Then more and more people came from England, from the potteries in the Midlands, and the work got more varied but more intense too. The end came for me when Austin decided to make salt and pepper pots. I had to make the holes with a nail!! I decided my future lay in another direction and handed in my notice.

Gillian Thomas née Stevenson

ಶ

My grandfather founded the Tea Works. My Dad was working there up to the Occupation but he didn't like the idea of leaving my mother all day at Samarès, whilst he was at First Tower, so he gave it up. I think they were making tomato soup during the Occupation. Not so long ago, before it closed down, my father's cousin Melville Walker was running it.

Senator Frank Walker

ಶ

When I joined the Overseas Trading Company in 1948 after service in the RAF, I started in the Accounts Department where there were about four staff. The total Office Staff consisted of about thirty employees engaged in Sales, Shipping, Buying, Accounts and a number of Secretaries.

In the factory there were about one hundred staff, mainly females engaged in tea packing and about twenty men including Engineers, Joiners, Warehousemen and Maintenance staff. The Chief Engineer was Bill McDowell and Joe Bryant was in charge of the Tea Loft where all the blending was done. Paul Le Maigat was in charge of Stocks of Materials

We too Remember When...

and Gordon Bewhay was the Foreman of the Dispatch Dept. I particularly remember Mr. Allbon, the Factory Manager, who always wore a black suit and bowler hat, also Mr Paul Dart who was in charge of the Joinery Dept. He was a cheerful character who always had a few words of advice for beginners like myself. I remember getting annoyed on occasions and he would say 'keep your powder dry son.' As time went on he was proved right many times!

I also remember Miss Una Querée who worked in the Factory Office and whose job it was to sound the factory hooter at 8 a.m., 1 p.m., 2 p.m., and 6 p.m. She was so conscientious in performing this task that many people living in the vicinity of First Tower would set their clocks by the Sun Works hooter. If through some oversight the hooter did not sound we would receive phone calls from people who thought their clocks had gone wrong!

When I started there were four Directors: Mr Melville Walker (Managing) Mr Helier Bisson (Company Secretary), Mr Bert Le Rossignol (Accountant) and Mr Victor Davis in charge of Administration.

We had an excellent Sports Pavilion built in the 1920's which is still in existence and is currently used by the Sun Bowls Club. In addition to the bowling green we had four tennis courts and in the early days, before television lured people away, we used to queue up for a game of tennis, playing perhaps once in an evening.

Until the early 1950's we would have an annual Sports Event on the beach at St. Ouen, near the Milano, when we would play cricket, have sack races etc. The Staff would all be taken out by coach and a high tea provided at the Milano at the end of the afternoon. This was discontinued probably due to the cost, with increases in the number of staff, and changing attitudes towards this type of function.

Every Christmas the staff were provided with an excellent festive lunch in the Staff canteen which was much appreciated and in the last seven years from Christmas 1985 a subsidized Christmas Dinner dance was also held, usually at the Pomme D'Or Hotel. This proved to be very popular and well supported until the closure of the company.

Bob Gallichan

Daff Noël

> The Overseas Trading Company had its own shop...

When I first took over the Staff Shop in 1976 it was for the O.T.C. Staff to buy tea bags and coffee at staff prices, also sweets and cigarettes. I was told I could sell what I liked and I did! I turned it into a mini market. I based it on the fact that the staff were working until 5 p.m. or later so would have difficulty in buying the necessities they may need such as toothpaste, soap, washing powder, tights, perfume etc. They would be able to buy a variety of goods from me during their breaks and at lunch time, as I was based in the Canteen which was very popular. The Canteen served good meals, and snacks, at subsidized prices and was a pleasant off-duty meeting place for the staff who would often sit on the veranda in fine weather and watch the bowlers, or just relax in the fresh air.

At Christmas, when necessary, I would be able to visit the wholesalers in between the factory breaks. All my wholesalers were very understanding and allowed me to buy in small quantities. I filled the shop with toys, cards, presents, in fact anything from tricycles to crackers.

Eileen Lees

Our Christmases were rather hard when I was a boy. On one of the best Christmases I can remember – I couldn't have been more than eight I suppose – we went out to visit my twin's godmother, Madame Glot. Unfortunately her husband had been killed in the First World War and, though she had two boys to bring up, I remember her pulling out this big tin bath filled with wooden toys, lorries and that sort of stuff. She was a lovely lady and very fond of Lester and myself.

Constable Bob Le Brocq

Our Christmases were wonderful! We had a routine that varied and changed as the years went on but, initially, there used to be parties on different days over Christmas, in the different family houses, and we used to play these silly games and eat ourselves to a standstill!

There was hardly any alcohol because my parents were effectively teetotal but they were wonderful warm occasions. They weren't massively wealthy by any means but they were comfortably off so that though they were very protective and worried about me, on the other hand they lavished things on me.

Senator Frank Walker

We too Remember When...

Remember when the Corbière train steamed noisily out of the dark St. Helier station into the blinding sunlight of a hot summer's day? How it rocked its way along the narrow lines, slowly enough for the passengers to read the bold adverts on the sheets of tin, fixed sturdily to the granite wall?

"Persil washes whiter! – Coleman's Mustard – Mazawatee Tea – Bovril Prevents That Sinking Feeling!" The last was my favourite. It featured the adventures of a man in his night shirt, hair spiked with fear, clinging to a giant jar of Bovril as he swirled in turbulent waters, away from danger, into a haven of unknown safety beyond the confines of the rectangle world he inhabited. It looked exciting!

Many were the halts along St. Aubin's Bay before, with a great sigh of despair, the engine began the slow, winding climb to Corbière Station. Our first trip of the year was always to Corbière, usually on the first warm spring Sunday. I'll never forget the surge of joy that swamped me as I climbed down onto the platform and stared towards the tiny lighthouse at the bottom of the steep hill. It was magical! As we walked down, the land got higher and the lighthouse bigger! By the time we reached the bottom the cliffs loomed up on either side and the enticing causeway dipped steeply before us.

On our return there would be plenty of time to cling to my Dad's hand and lean adventurously over the causeway edge to search out the dog-fish stranded in the between-tide pools. Maybe we'd climb some of the great rocks ... but now! ... Now there was but one aim, to march boldly along the beckoning causeway until we reached the object of our journey ... the lighthouse ... stretched to the sky ... enormous!

At the end of the afternoon, flasked tea and paste sandwiches having met their destined end while we rested on a convenient rock, we started the painful climb back to the station. My Mum found the walk difficult because she had rheumatism so Dad carried all the paraphernalia, even Mum's handbag!

The train would be waiting, its boiler fussily releasing steam as if impatient with our slowness, then quickly purchased ice-cream in hand, I'd settle next to my Dad in the cosy carriage. We'd rock back to town at an alarming speed, Dad's exaggerated lurching sending me into fits of half fearful giggles until we got back to St. Helier and walked, tired and happy, back to our home at the Museum.

Mary Connell née Clements born 1929

I remember the lighthouse keepers at Corbière, Joe Shenton in particular. I knew him well because we had, what was then, a summer bungalow at Corbière. The men lived in the little cottages above the causeway and there was a tea-room place where the bus from town stopped. We used to use those tea-rooms a lot. I was a kid in those years, of course, before the lighthouse went automatic.

If I want to wrestle with a major problem, or sort out my brain, I'll go and sit on a rock at Corbière. I've got a favourite rock there. I might sit there for an hour, maybe two hours, occasionally even longer, and just think things through. There's something about Corbière that sets it apart.

Senator Frank Walker

I remember we used to have a bungalow on Gorey Common and, though one wouldn't want to wish them back because they were pretty ugly, in those days people didn't go away on holiday like they do now and it was the highlight of our family weekends during the summer. It was very simple, a couple of little bunk beds, a living room, a veranda and a Valor stove. My mother would insist that as it was Sunday we had to have a roast joint even if we were out there. My brothers would dig a big hole on the beach, put an umbrella over it and that would be mine. Geoffrey's little house. Perhaps we would walk to Seymour Tower if the tide was low and get razor fish and try and flog them around the other bungalows. Those were lovely days.

Reverend Geoffrey Baker

In those days nearly everyone had weekend bungalows or chalets in different bays and everybody went there. It wasn't a case that you had to be posh to have one. My parents had a bungalow at Ouaisné, it was just a corrugated iron one, we used to go there every weekend.

Alicia Priddy

I can remember how we left our front door open all night, it was never locked. We used to go on the beach all day and leave the door wide open. Nobody ever came. We were safe. We never questioned it.

Jill De Sousa

We too Remember When...

One thing that has changed a lot is the amount of traffic on the roads. When I was at St. Michaels I used to bicycle to school at the age of nine or ten. This was a three or four mile ride across some major roads, but there was never much traffic around that I can remember. Now I would be very hesitant about allowing a young child of mine to cycle along all these roads. All the roads, which were once lanes, have now got great big indentations where cars have squeezed past each other.

Sir Phillip Bailhache

Do you remember when it was common for men and boys to whistle as they went about their day? Very often it was catching, setting one humming the melody long after. Once, as I walked passed the Piggeries, I heard a young woman singing. Through the window I could see her scrubbing the kitchen table and recognised her as one of the older girls of a large family who lived in the area. I remember joining in and was still singing when I reached my aunt's house some distance away. Nobody thought anything of it though I passed several people on the way.

Another time, as I was returning home from some errand, I saw a girl dancing her way along the pavement of Beresford Street oblivious of all but her imaginary audience. There were only a few people about but those that were stopped and smiled as she went by. Yet she was quite unaware of them.

Daff Noël

Lady Anne Wilkes, née Huelin, *wife of His Excellency the Lieutenant-Governor, General Sir Michael Wilkes, was born in England, during Dunkirk Week...*

I spent the five years of the war down in Devon with my mother and grandparents. My father was captured in Dunkirk and held prisoner for the whole of the war. He studied farming during that time and, when he came back to Jersey after the Occupation, he reared Jersey cows in St. Peters. I was brought back by Granny Huelin straight after the war. We lived at The Garth.

I can remember quite a lot of things from those early days especially the first oranges we were given. We sat at the bottom of the garden, sucking these oranges with a lump of sugar stuck in the top! I have a very vivid memory of that which made me realise that we didn't have sweets then. There was rationing for quite a long time and when sweets did come in, the shops began to have wonderful things....Easter eggs with your own name on them!...Gob stoppers! Do you remember them? You don't see those nowadays.

The other thing I recall was the complete freedom we enjoyed during the holidays. I grew up with quite a lot of friends my own age in St. Peter's and we could roam around on our bikes, or with ponies, sometimes with a picnic in hand. The only rule we had was that we weren't to swim in the sea unattended, which left us a lot of scope!

My friends all lived nearby and we could do lots of things on our own, whereas children today have to be escorted everywhere. Old Major De Gruchy's grandchildren who lived at Les Hurreaux, which was just into St. Ouen's at the top of Val de la Mare now, were great friends. Their parents were in India so they were brought up by their grandparents and a nanny. They had their own large playroom run by 'nanny' and their own territory with a courtyard to play in. We had wonderful, wonderful times romping and playing mah-jong.

There were about five of us that would gather together in the holidays. We cycled quite a long way, always with picnics of doughnuts, sandwiches, well, doorstops, and warm orange squash! We didn't have cooler bags! We'd go down Grève de Lecq, the sand dunes at St. Ouens. We'd climb into the German Underground Hospital which, of course, would have been terribly frowned upon. We wound up the air conditioning and romped around inside there and nobody ever knew!

My cousin Nigel and I, our friends the Richardson girls, and sometimes one or two others that we cut in on our escapades, were all equal to thinking up devilment. We had lots of time, with no television, to plan mischief. It's really quite frightening to think what we got up to!

I had a very good childhood, very happy when I think about it, definite shades of Enid Blyton. As I said there was absolute freedom and nobody worried about the traffic or 'strange' people. Everybody knew who the 'strange' were and would keep an eye on them. New faces were rare.

I had a girl friend, Jane, whose parents were abroad. She spent quite a lot of her holidays with me after about the age of nine, nine 'til sixteen. In those days, if the parents worked abroad you weren't flown out for the holidays so she stayed with me and we shared a room that was otherwise, being that much older than my brother and sister, solely mine.

We too Remember When...

Jane and I were part of the gang getting up to mischief. We still keep in touch with each other.

We all used to go over the cliffs at Crabbé and swim in the pool down below. There's a very deep, sea-water pool... it's got a name but I don't know it. But that wasn't in the sea, you see, so again we children could do some naughty things without totally disobeying the rules! Do you know that at Grève De Lecq there's a tunnel through the cliff? At low tide you can go through to the next bay, but only at low tide. You have to go quite a long way down, and move quite quickly to get there and back, but we used to do that quite regularly, every holiday. That was just one of the really naughty things we did!

I could swim quite well because Granny Huelin took me to Havre des Pas, aged seven, to learn. It was bitterly cold – always! And those crocodiles in the bottom – with the big seaweed streamers floating around! Everybody remembers swimming there more than anything else I think. Horrendous!

My birthday was always in the summer half term and we used to have a big picnic down at Val De La Mare which is now, of course, the reservoir. (My father owned the land then, he sold it to make the reservoir.) All our friends would join us and we'd play hide and seek in the completely wild valley. There was a sort of railway line going down it, all covered up with brambles. The Germans must have built it, don't know quite for what or why! There were no cottages down there, only Greenlands, the farm, on the top. It was great fun and, then again, the sense of freedom that the young can't have nowadays.

There was lots of land and space – brambles, wild daffodils, blackberries. We were paid sixpence a pound for picking blackberries, by my mother. We thought that was lovely!

I'm the eldest in the family because the war intervened and my brother and sister were born afterwards. We have a half brother by my father's second marriage. We're all over here now so that's rather nice. Our parents were very strict. We were expected to be seen and not heard. You didn't speak until you were spoken to, and you only had lunch with your parents, no other meal. Always. You were kept away in the nursery. Father was very Victorian. We put our parents on pedestals, still do, grandparents desperately so.

I remember Granny Huelin very well, my father's mother. Being the eldest I was very spoilt by the grandparents, nobody else. I used to be taken out on my own, looking nice. She would take me to tea at Gaudins after the cinema. Do you remember Gaudins and that lovely three-tiered cake stand, the silver service... and their toasted teacakes? Sometimes my cousin Nigel would come too and we could always have as much as we liked. We were very spoilt. We used to go quite often to the cinema too. Remember the organ at the Forum that used to come up and we used to sing? And Wests Cinema? Apart from these trips we weren't taken out much. We'd have friends to stay but we weren't taken out very often by my parents. We had to make our own amusement.

There's still nothing quite like shrimping at Fliquet! We'd follow the tide down with our nets and catch proper shrimps then, big ones. I don't think you'd find them in the pools now – the pollution, I suppose. I remember cockling with Granny Huelin at St. Aubin's, we had them cooked after. They tasted so good! Oh! and I recall we went to Herm one day for somebody's birthday party. They hired a big motor boat! That was very exciting!

I remember helping my father's cowman with the cows and showing them at Springfield. My father's cows showed very successfully. They were lovely cows, much paler than they are today, much creamier in colour. I didn't work, just played around the farm as part of the holiday's activities. I loved it but it would never have been allowed for me to milk the cows. I fetched the milk for the house though, going down to the shed with the jug. I remember the butter we made in the house, with an old butter churn, and the old machinery on the farm, the chopping of

Anne Huelin showing one of her father's cows.

the hay for the cows. You pushed it up one end, and you turned, and they chopped it like that. The same with the mangle-wurzels. Such dangerous machinery! All unprotected, because there were no guards around mechanisms in those days. They'd be all museum pieces now, if they still existed.

The workers were French and they lived in the outbuilding, awful really. They had a barrel of cider and were paid the day they went back to France, so that the money got back to their families. I can't remember how many we had but I do remember them. I remember the harvesting of the grain with an enormous big stationary carbine, which was brought to the farm, and bringing all the hay back on horse-drawn carts. We didn't have horses of our own so they must have been part of the equipment that moved around from farm to farm, along with the threshing machine, during harvesting. I remember playing in the stooks, which were put up like little teepees in those days, and taking out lunch for the workers, and everyone sitting around with you.

We had a goat to trim the hedges for *branchage* and I remember deciding to take the goat for a walk. Of course it was off like grease lightning. Ah! The catch! I was sent to my room yet again! I was regularly sent to my room in disgrace! My biggest misdemeanour was climbing in the haylofts. It was forbidden because the floor was so unsafe. I was up there with my cousin Nigel and he fell through, landing inches from the horns of one of the cows. That wasn't well received, there's no doubt about that! He was fine, but a few inches in the other direction and he'd have been on the horns!

Apart from perhaps a bridesmaid's dress that was worn for parties we had very drab clothes, the same as our parents but made smaller. I had a knitted swimsuit and, when it was wet, it hanged! What they inflicted on us! The bubbly elasticated ones that came out later were much better. I remember going to Beghins for our shoes three times a year, wearing them home, and being told not to scuff them because they had to last! If you outgrew your sandals you simply cut a hole across the toes, and wore them like that until you could have some new ones. I was lucky as the eldest, because I had a few new things, but my mother was very good at making things from anything, which could be awful. If there was a dress she no longer wore she just altered it!

We had sixpence a week pocket money but my friend Jane and I would go out on our bicycles to collect bottles to take to the village shop and get tuppence back on each one. We were very clever at it! We covered all the beaches and made quite a tidy bit of money, which we spent on books mostly. Books and sweets. My favourite reading? Oh! as a child, Enid Blyton, definitely, and the *Girl, Eagle* and *School Friend* comics. The comics weren't delivered. We had to go to the shop at the top of Jubilee Hill. The airport wasn't so busy then. We used to go mushrooming there! There are a lot more buildings than there used to be, but St. Peters still has a village atmosphere.

One thing that I reckon has been to our benefit today has been the creation of the cliff paths; it was hard work getting anywhere as a child! We were quite different children from today's youngsters. We had to make our own fun. I spent a simple childhood, with lots of friends that I still meet now. It was idyllic and I look back on it with great pleasure.

❧

I have reached my eighty-third year but can recall my childhood years most vividly (although if you were to ask me what I did last week I truthfully could not remember!)

I was five years older than my brother, and *because* he was a boy he got off very lightly. I used to have to clean his shoes, which always infuriated me. I found that so unfair! Also he could 'go out and play' but there was always a job for 'Doris to do', mainly because I was 'only a girl'. My maternal grandparents lived with us and were bed-ridden. It was a lot of hard work, especially for Mum who would attend to their needs before leaving for her work. When I returned home from school I used to see to their needs, like giving them a hot drink or making them a sandwich, till Mum returned home and would give them a 'proper' tea. Mum never had much time to sit down. As soon as Dad returned from work his meal would be placed in front of him, nothing exotic like steak but I can still recall the succulent smell of the lovely soup or stew. Mum rarely sat at the table with us as most of the cooking was done on an open range and had to be constantly attended by adding twigs, or using the bellows if it didn't 'draw' properly. After our meal Mum would 'relax' and do whatever mending needed doing. The days she disliked most were 'when the wind was in the wrong direction' and smuts would be everywhere. On a 'good' day, when the grate was burning brightly, she would bring out her lily-white washing and iron it with a small iron. Our sheets were enormous (or so it seemed to me) and as white as snow. She was very proud of 'a job well done!' Another of her favourite jobs was

We too Remember When...

polishing the lamps so that we could have a 'good' light to darn Dad's socks by!

For many years Mum and Dad saved every penny that they could to buy me a piano. It was an ambition of mine to 'play the piano' and I eventually spent hours at the keyboard. On reflection I value it even more now. Mum and Dad *never* bought anything for themselves. It was always Charlie and I who mattered. Another 'sacrifice' was that at Christmas time we always had something in our stocking, a bar of chocolate, a small toy etc., etc. My mother joined a Christmas Club paying in what she could afford each week and Christmas week she would draw it out and buy Charlie and me our Christmas present. What a different world we live in today!

Nothing was ever wasted in our house. It was considered 'a sin' to throw food away etc. Mum taught me how to sew and mend and how to darn Dad and Charlie's socks. I recall very clearly the day Mum told Dad, 'Doris needs a new dress.' I was very big for my age and after a lot of thought Dad said I could have one made by a lady seamstress who lived nearby. On one condition though. It had to last a long time and be *reversible*! My Mum quaked at the thought of asking the dressmaker if this was possible but this very clever lady said it was, so Mum bought the material. I can still see it today, a lovely soft material, dark red in colour. And the fittings that followed! During the week, at school, I wore it on the reverse side and on Sunday, for Church, I wore it on the 'right' side! Can you imagine anyone doing that today? I *never* told anyone about my 'inside/out' dress, but the object of telling you is to explain how we were known to be *les pauvres.*

My brother needed new shoes and Dad decided to eat humble pie and see if Charlie could have some Westaway boots. Charlie was furious and refused to wear them but of course my father took no notice of that and insisted that they were worn 'or else!' Reluctantly my brother wore them but when out of sight of our home he would take them off. From then on it was all systems go! He would take out an old, very tattered, pair of plimsolls (or sand-shoes as they were then) from the hedge and replace the dreaded Westaways in the same hiding place before skipping gaily to school. His class teacher scolded him for coming to school 'with those awful shoes'.

Unfortunately one day Charlie was 'kept in' and so, not wanting to return home late, he just hurried back forgetting that he had the tattered shoes on. My father noticed that immediately and demanded an

Daff Noël

explanation. He was not amused! Charlie had to apologise to the teacher, collect the boots from their hiding place and wear them. The sand-shoes were never seen again *and* Charlie had to keep to the straight and narrow for a very long time afterward! Strange how all the children *dreaded* Westaway boots, for that is what was given out then for both sexes in those days!

Finally, one of my favourite memories of my schooldays was seeing 'the kitchen chimney smoke' as I turned the corner. That meant that Mum was home and the fire would be lit and a nice hot drink would be waiting for us. It was a wonderful feeling and a memory I shall always treasure.

Doris Le Mercier, *born 1916*

Mrs Iris De La Mare née Morris *was born in 1916 too...*

I was born in, I'm fairly sure, our house in Old St. John's Road. My father died when I was eight. He was a porter on the Jersey Railway. Six foot he was. Lovely man, quiet, gentle. My mother was wonderful, yes wonderful. She married again, once we were all married, Ernest Beuzeval. Another gentle soul, he was absolutely wonderful. We called him 'Pop'. He'd have done anything for us. That was fortunate, eh?

I had a sister Ruby who married Percy Landick and had the Newsagent in Rouge Bouillon. She died of cancer at 60. She was the eldest, then two years later there was my brother George, then there was seven years before I came along. My brother ended up working at the Penny Savings Bank. He died at the age of 87. Was I spoilt being the baby? No, not really, though they said I was! They said, "She gets away with it, Mum!"

It was a very happy home. As you went in the front door you had our kitchen and a little room that led off that was a bedroom. Then on the other side of the passage was what we called the sitting room. Upstairs were two more bedrooms and a box room. There was a street lamp outside which shone into our bedroom. The lamp-lighter used to come around to put it on and off. There was a little garden out the back and a cellar underneath the house, where my mother used to take in washing. I knocked at the door a few years ago and I said to the lady,

"You don't mind me being rude but I used to live here, have you got the cellar underneath there still?"

We too Remember When...

I won't tell you the swear word she used but she said, "That so and so's still there!!"

Where did we play? In the road. Yes! We did! Remember the Aberfeldy Hotel? They had a green in front and we used to go up there and play... Yes! We used to play Tin Pot Monkey... well, that was mostly when we went down on the People's Park. How did we play it? Well you got a tin in the middle and one of the children had their eyes closed while everybody scattered. When he was looking he'd call out,

"Look out! Look out! The monkey's on the watch!"

Then it was a case of creeping back in to kick the tin without that child seeing. I can remember it as if it was yesterday. Oh! It was fun!

All our friends lived in the area you see and we all met up on the park. There were no swings there then. I remember the yards of cottages that lined Westmount Road, with the outside pumps and lines of washing. Living in Old St. John's Road we used to go down a lane that went passed the houses, where our friends lived, to get to the park. Lovely long gardens they had. Another thing we used to do is pitch a tent in the middle of their garden and play 'Tents'. Also we got up concerts, loads of concerts. We sang and danced, "I'm forever blowing bubbles...", wearing dresses that we'd made out of crêpe paper, and we charged, probably a half-penny a time, to come in. Ah! Yes!

On Saturday mornings The Tin House had 'Go As You Please' competitions. So what we did, three of us, we thought we'd enter. After school we'd come home and we'd start thinking of what we were going to do. One of the girl's fathers had a garage in Seale Street and he said we

Iris with two friends, Rosa and Freda Rickett.

could practise in there. We went in the competition and we sang 'Connie In The Cornfield' and did a little shuffle and we came second! It was great fun! You see there were loads of things you could do.

Later on I went to Miss Larcombe, on the corner which is the Wellington Hall now, she ran a little dancing school. We put on a concert at Springfield, yes, on the stage there. I was a hula-hula girl. My mother had to put all this raffia on a band, you know, and make a chain of poppies.

'Course you had Sunday School treats in the horse and van. Oh! Yes! When I was very, very small I went to St. Andrews, which doesn't exist now, on the Esplanade. My brother was in the choir. But then it became obsolete so St. Andrews was moved to First Tower. My brother went there but it was too far for me, I was too little. Eventually I ended up at All Saints and we had great times. Also, don't forget, years ago the Sunday School picnics used to go on the train to Gorey and have races on the Common.

There seemed to be so much, but you see people today are far too busy. There are dancing schools and a lot going on, but it doesn't seem to be quite the same. It seems to be too competitive now.

Were my parents strict? My mother more than my father, yes. He left it to my mother and she would, yes. But we never had the cane – her voice was enough to frighten us! But she was lovely.

What sort of chores did I have to do in the home? My brother and sister said I never done any! They had to do the beds and little bits but they said I got away with it! Obviously I did, I'm sure I did, being seven years between us you know. And of course, I tell you what, after the war, the first one, there was that terrible epidemic. It was world-wide but I can't remember what it was but anyway I went down with it and I was very, very ill. I was unconscious and they didn't think I'd live. So I never looked well. I was always 'delicate' but really I was strong. (Touch wood, I keep fabulous.) But being like that then, I was very, very pale. My friends used to call me 'foul neck' and 'tin ribs' because I was extremely thin. I didn't mind though, I joined in with everything. I was just sickly looking and couldn't put on weight.

We moved eventually to St. Simon's Church in Great Union Road. There were two cottages in the yard; Mrs Raffray, the caretaker lived in the other. My mother used to help putting chairs and things in the hall. Both cottages have gone now. I can remember them being just ordinary, no mod cons obviously. The black range in the kitchen, a scullery. A tin bath of course.

We too Remember When...

Do you know, when I cleared my brother's cottage after his death in 1996 he still had his tin bath! He'd been in his cottage fifty years and there were no mod cons in it at all. Just one cold water tap! But he loved it, adored it. He wouldn't have moved. 87 he was when he died. He was healthy, no problems.

It's this central heating that's bad for you, you know. I've noticed it since I've moved into this lovely flat. I've never had central heating before, ever. Mind you I don't put all the radiators on even now.

When I left school, at fourteen, you could leave school right after your birthday. You didn't have to stay until the end of the term. I didn't have a job, but my mother's sister had a friend who had a big greengrocers on the corner of Conway Street, so I started there. I didn't like it but you couldn't leave your job, especially with your mother being a widow – you needed the money – so I went to the Tea Stores at First Tower. I cycled there and the weather sometimes when you went by the Pavilion! Anyway I went there packing the teas and doing the chores. In those days they had their quiet spells and one day Mr Holmen came to us and said, "I'm sorry I've got to put some of you down," and being one of the last ones in, well I had to go. Mr Holmen was a lovely gentleman, very religious.

So I found a job waitressing to a little café at Havres Des Pas. I was a bit nervous but the lady who owned it was charming. She told me to shut up in my lunch hour and go for a swim, which I used to do. I used to go across to the pool.

After the summer Mr Holmen came to our house and asked if I'd like to go back, they were busy. So back I went and what happened again? Yes. There came a slack time!

Now my mother used to do washing for Mrs Brookes, who had the newsagent in King Street where my sister had worked for years. So one day when I was taking the laundry back I asked Mrs Brookes if she had a job. She didn't give me an answer right away but when my sister came back in the evening she said I could start. Wonderful people. Mrs Brookes was a widow and she had four boys, Wally, Cyril, Charlie and Ted.

The King Street shop was very nice. We sold books, papers, photo frames and such. At first Brookes were the agents for newspapers, before Whites, so that was a very busy time because we had to set up the rounds. Do you remember Lord Porthsea? His sister used to live here? Well, one day I happened to look at the English papers just before his chauffeur came in and asked if we knew which paper had reported that Lord Porthsea had been made a Member of Parliament for Portsmouth. I said

Daff Noël

Iris alongside the 'Newspaper Stand' at West Park.

'Yes! I did' and sold it to him. Lord Porthsea's sister was in the car parked outside and she sent the chauffeur back in with five shillings for me!

Brookes had another shop in Bath Street as well. It faced Belmont Road. That was a very old shop and we used to have to go up and clean it. Did I mind doing the cleaning when I was employed as a shop assistant? Oh! God no! We'd have done anything. God yes, no problem. We cleaned and dressed the window, oh! yes! How much did I get paid? I think I ended up with £2.10s when I got married. I was twenty-four years of age.

I was younger than twenty when I met my husband at a dinner dance. I didn't fall in love with him straight away though he was a very gentle, quiet man. We were courting quite a while when we got engaged, well, we never had the money. When we went to the pictures we each had to pay for our own! When we first met he worked as a furniture remover, so he didn't earn much money. He was one of seven, so he had to give his money into his home.

We were married. Well, you're not going to believe this but we were furnishing a nice little house in Rouge Bouillon, next door to my sister's paper shop, when the war started. It had taken us a long time to do it up and buy furniture, especially on our wages, and with my mother being a

We too Remember When...

widow, and him having to contribute to his family as well... and remember we weren't even living in it because in those days you didn't live together before you were married! We'd been so happy gradually getting things for it. I had a bottom drawer of course and in those days parents were strict on good linen, so I got some from the Universal Club which my brother ran. I don't think I ever had to buy linen again in my life because I had a box full of linen. It was all pure cotton and so hard wearing. Lasted a life time.... Well, to get back to what I was telling you, there were notices saying that the Germans were coming and though I queued outside the Town Hall I didn't get away. So then I started to think about our little house and how we'd lose everything if they billeted the Germans there and I decided we'd get married.

So I went to my husband at his work, and told him, and he said I'd have to arrange it all. I went straight to the Dean and explained, and he said that after all the years we'd been saving he could tell it wasn't a spur of the moment thing, so he would marry us at half past seven that evening. Unbelievable eh?

Well, I was working for Brookes so I went and explained and they said, "You'd better have the time off to do all your bits." I asked them if they would make it to the wedding and they said yes. I went across to Chings in Broad Street. It was really busy with people buying to stock up, so I said to my friend, who was serving,

"Let me have a pair of navy court shoes size five, when you have a minute eh? I'm getting married tonight."

I didn't even try them on, just paid my money. Then I went to Frederick Bakers and chose a hat to match the shoes.

After that I went down to the harbour to see my husband who was moving furniture to safety after the bombing and told him we were getting married at 7.30 p.m. I can see his face now!

"I don't think I can make it!" he said, (sounds like a comic opera doesn't it? but it's true!)

"Well," I said, "You'd better. I've arranged it all like you said!"

I had to phone my brother who'd gone back to work after his lunch to ask him if he'd give me away and he said yes, that was all right. No problem. I went to Gaudins. They only had a bit of wedding cake left, but I had what she had, and my cousin gave me two bottles of wine. I ordered the taxies and then I went home to get ready.

I was at the Church first, because my husband's taxi went to Don Road instead of Don Street, where he lived, so we had to drive around

Daff Noël

Iris and her husband.

the church until he arrived! I honestly couldn't tell you who was in the Church. The Best Man couldn't make it so somebody stood in. I had my blue dress but because of all the rush we didn't get many wedding presents and there were no bridesmaids or proper photographs.

We had a little get-together at my home then we went back to our house, but it was very strange because I was used to having my family around me, and my husband had been living with his parents. To tell you the truth when I shut the door I felt very strange. I felt cut off. I felt quite lonely. Strange...

We'd been married eighteen years when he died of cancer.

ða

Les Le Ruez *was born at Westfield, St. Mary in 1932 and has lived there all his life...*

The parish has not changed much in those years, there's been building yes but it's not been overdone. Mostly the developments have been for people with very strong connections with the parish. We've lost a lot of the farms of course, that's probably the biggest change. There were forty-five or fifty when I was growing up but now I think there are about eight or ten left. A lot of the farms have been broken up obviously and the land has been taken over by others. I've been involved in Parish life since I was twenty-three. I love the Parish and wouldn't dream of living anywhere else.

I went to quite a number of little private schools when I was growing up. My very first school was Homestead, St. Peter and my teacher was Nan Le Ruez. I then went to another small private school in St. Mary where the tutor was Miss Ouless, sister of the Reverend Ouless. The actual place where she had this classroom was across the road from the Rectory, in the property known as 'L'Anciente.'

By this time we had reached the Occupation and I was sent to another private school in St. Ouen's which was run by a Mr and Mrs Tolk. They were Dutch, a Dutch couple who spoke fluent German, and I learnt quite a lot of the language from them. Well, I was there for two and a half years when my father decided I should go to Victoria College (this was probably a waste of his money but still I went!) Now the teaching of German was compulsory during the Occupation and the result was that at the end of the first term, there was a prize giving and to my amazement I found I was first in the class. Now under different circumstances one would have been pleased with what one had done but because we were under German occupation I was absolutely disgusted and ashamed. I cycled back home here with the book on the back of the bike, tore it up and burned it. As far as I was concerned I'd done a terrible thing in winning that prize.

I remained at the College until 1946. I wasn't too unhappy to be leaving for I can't say I was any great scholar, I was much happier on the farm. I never liked sport and used to skip it to come home and work on the farm. I was never found out either!

My father died in 1949, when I was seventeen, and at that age you're not really as responsible as you should be to run a farm. I had no option but to go ahead as best I could. It was made somewhat complicated by some well meaning relatives thinking I should expand on the cattle and others saying I should go more on the potatoes, so it was a difficult period not knowing which way to go. Then I was grabbed by a young lady from Rozel, who fortunately became my wife. But even once we were married we remained undecided which way we were going with the farm. Things were very hard financially at first.

I did expand on the potatoes quite a bit and the result was in 1956 we had a very bad season. The whole crop was frozen. I was only getting half-a-crown a hundredweight down the Weighbridge. That wasn't a lot of money and it rather disgusted us. However, in the meantime, because of the unreliable seasons, a cousin of Mazel's had started to take in guests so we decided to follow and that's how our guest-house began, albeit in a small way.

We took five guests the first year, carried on with less potatoes but the same amount of cattle, and went on the following year to get the place registered. We could then take eight. Bit by bit we expanded on that, still doing the potatoes for another two years before we gave them up.

My mother was still living in the wing and she had another couple of rooms that she didn't really need so that took us gradually to ten. It was proving quite remunerative obviously so we decided to just continue with the cattle. We built an extra room on the end of the house, adjoining the bathroom, whilst at the same time – because one of the sheds had become redundant – we turned the potato loft into a flat and let that on a permanent lease. Two years later we took another plunge and built another flat beneath that one. So we now had two on permanent lease.

We carried on with just the cattle – we had fourteen or fifteen milkers that's all – for another four years before I eventually decided that there was no point in carrying on. They weren't paying and we were tied, unable to go away. So we gave them up, I suppose to certain people's disgust for it didn't go down too well but there you are. It was our business and nobody else's.

Then we took a third plunge, built another bedroom which took four, and this brought us up to fifteen guests. It remained in that situation until six or seven years ago when we refurbished the dower cottage at great expense and it's now let as self-catering. (It's where my mother had originally lived and what had since been used as a storeroom.) We'd also built an extra store alongside the old stable and that's been let for a number of years. So due to a combination of things, we've adapted our farm so that it continues to give us a living.

It's been hard work but nevertheless it was very worthwhile and slowly we've been able to enjoy life a bit more. I must say though, that with all that we've done, we've never borrowed a penny. That is probably very unusual. I realise now that we could probably have done all that we have very much quicker, and been better off, if we'd had the nerve to borrow – but one hadn't been brought up to borrow.

We've never been afraid to help each other either inside or out. Mazel was brought up on a farm so she has always been willing to do her bit,

We too Remember When...

and more. I help Mazel of course. I Hoover and 'feed' the dishwasher and yes, at first it was difficult because of course it was not what I was brought up to. In our time men worked outside on the farm and the women took care of the house. In fact it was rather looked down upon, for the men to help out, but it was the way we had to do things. We were taking a gamble, one that paid off – albeit not immediately. It was not something that happened overnight, in fact we weren't able to go on holiday until we gave up the cattle.

In our young days all the courting was done on Sunday evenings by driving along the roads from Bethlehem Chapel to St. John's Church, down to St. Lawrence Church, up again to Trinity Church and from Trinity Church to St. Martin's. It was a rat run for motor bikes and cars. That's how you met the girls – and, it's true, they went to all those churches on the route to meet us! I went to Bethlehem Chapel and Mazel went to Carmel, but because none of the young men went down Carmel on a Sunday the girls used to pretend they wanted to go to Trinity Church so that they could walk all the way back! That's the way we all met up.

I had a car, a Vauxhall. It had been my dad's originally but then after that car I went mad. I can't remember how many cars I had afterwards!

How did I meet Mazel? Well, we actually met at a Young Farmers Bonfire Night, at Jardin D'Olivet, in 1949. I was going to the Bonfire Night organised by the Young Farmers Club and Len Picot and myself schemed up this jape (we were always mucking about, Len and me) but, as it so happens, an elderly relative of mine died a couple of days before. So my mother said,

"You can't go out tonight. You've got to stay inside!"

I thought, 'how am I going to work this one?' and I came up with this story that there was a business meeting. So I went out all dressed up in collar and tie for this business meeting, met Len Picot at his home, Hautville, went in the stable and changed into my old clothes!

Now Len's brother had just taken a delivery of a reconditioned pre-war Bedford lorry which we'd decided to use and we put a tank with a stirrup pump in the back before setting off. Nobody heard the lorry go. We let it freewheel down the small incline of Hautville's backyard and off we went.

When we got to the bonfire we found the huge heap of *vauxpas* (husks), from the threshing machine of Don Pallot's, which one of us suggested was on fire. I drove the lorry around like an absolute lunatic whilst one of the lads in the back with the stirrup pump pretended to put it out!

Daff Noël

Unfortunately we were right into the heap when we nearly got stuck. How we failed to set the whole thing alight I don't know!

Eventually we got back to Hautville and put the lorry away with no one any the wiser. We changed into our suits and went on to the dance at the Young Farmers' Headquarters where Len, shall we say, negotiated an introduction on my behalf with this attractive young lady, Mazel De Gruchy. I took her home in the Vauxhall. I drove, as usual, like a maniac and Mazel was not impressed. She says now that she hung on to the seat, and that if anything had happened the seat would have gone with her! She was that terrified. She said she would 'never go out with me again'. 'Sarcastic Le Ruez' she called me. So that evening didn't materialise into anything at all.

It was quite some time afterwards, probably a year or so, that I found out via the grapevine, that Mazel had finished with a long standing boyfriend so I went down, outside her family farm, Carmel, at Rozel and put my hand on the hooter and kept it there! Her father wasn't too happy but she came out and I made a date for the following day, Easter Monday, the day of the Hill Climb. And that was the fateful day. We've never looked back since.

We were both twenty when we married and I wasn't allowed to wander again. We had a lovely country wedding at Trinity Church and our reception was at the Ritz Hotel, in Colomberie. It was a beautiful reception. We managed to go away, on honeymoon. By that time I had a Sunbeam Talbot and we toured Cornwall and Devon and the Lake District. It was the first time I'd been away with the car and of course it had to go on the traditional cargo boat. The car went ahead in those days and you picked it up at the docks. Ah! No, we didn't go with the car. We went by air. We had a lovely time but things didn't go well on our return. We came back overnight on the boat with the car and, as we were coming into St. Helier, I was just thinking of having a cup of coffee and a piece of toast when I found out I couldn't. Mazel hadn't slept too well and she'd given one of the stewards, who'd been very kind to her, the last half-crown we had left! We landed with nothing!

We too Remember When...

> Les's wife, **Jurat Mazel Le Ruez née De Gruchy** was born, the eldest of five girls, at La Franchise, St. Martin...

When I was six months old my father went back to his old family home, Carmel Farm, at Rozel and we lived in the cottage belonging to it. When my grandfather built his own house, and moved further up the hill, we moved into the farm itself. So that's where I was brought up.

Carmel Farm was next door to the chapel. Sadly Carmel Chapel doesn't exist any more but being right next door to our farm we attended there regularly. It was a tiny little chapel with a harmonium and a little stage. I sang my first solo on that stage during the Anniversary:

'Little birds are singing in the leafy trees.
Little flowers are waving in the gentle breeze'

I was four years old! What was I wearing? Probably a Shirley Temple dress. I remember I had a little frilly bonnet!

Dad was one of these people who believed that you didn't just buy a lot of clothes. You bought clothes to last. As children we were dressed like Shirley Temple, who was the darling, curly-haired child film star of the time. We had 'Shirley Temple' dresses. We didn't have them very often but they lasted and they were beautiful. Dad always made sure we were nicely dressed. The building that was once Carmel Chapel is a private home now. It's changed dramatically.

My parents had a great faith but they didn't 'throw it around'. We had a Christian upbringing. We were always taught to say our prayers when we went to bed and even though my dad was a strong man he said his prayers every night. He wasn't a big churchgoer but he had his faith. Yes, I looked over the little ones as they said their baby prayers. Our Christian faith was the foundation of our home and we always gave thanks before every meal.

When we girls were older we went on from Carmel to Trinity Church, and not only for the boys – though it was said to be one of the reasons! I liked going to Church as well! But yes, we used to walk, two or three girls, to and from the Church to see the boys. I remember once we were coming out of church and there was this car load of boys that we weren't particularly fond of and we ran into this turnip field to escape them, in our Sunday best! In those days one wore hats and white shoes, so you can imagine it. Girls today have lost that innocent fun.

There's seventeen months between my next sister Maureen and me, then there was a break of six years (for mother lost a little boy in between) before Jean arrived, then Marjorie and Shirley with fourteen and sixteen months between them. So, of course, with being the eldest I changed their nappies many times! I had to help on the farm too.

We started school at a little farm next door with Miss Valpy. She was only young. Her elder sister Monica was courting Reg Jeune and my sister and I used to watch them both, peeping from behind the hedge! We thought it was lovely. Anyhow, we started at Miss Valpy and afterwards we went on to Trinity School.

It was a good school with many classes for there was a full range of ages because, of course, you didn't leave to go on to Senior school in those days. Though I loved it in the infants department, I wasn't happy at Trinity School. The Headmaster, Mr Ingram, was quite a character. Not the nicest man possible. He had a bad leg and he used to put this leg out purposefully so that you would trip over it and give him cause to reprimand you. We were terrified of him.

I must admit I was pleased to leave and go to the Girls' Collegiate School, during the Occupation, even though we had to cycle there, all the way from Rozel, on hard tyres! But towards the end of the Occupation, when things were quite bad, we used to stay the school week in town, at a cousin of my Dad's, Mrs Le Masurier, returning home for the weekend.

The Collegiate was a lovely school. I always believed there was a tunnel in the cellars. A few of us used to go down to the cellars and pick at what we thought was a covered doorway. We always believed it hid a passage that had been sealed off but we never had a chance to investigate further.

Yes, as I said, it was a lovely school. There was the Headmistress, Miss Clough, she was still at the helm until she was nearly ninety I think, and Miss Hoskins. She had white hair and was a wonderful woman. Their aim was to make ladies out of us. They taught us manners and how to lead a decent life. We also had Miss Le Feuvre, who was the French teacher, she was super, Miss Gayford, she was a lovely person as well, and of course Miss Kathleen Hunt. She was the one who started the Guide Company. She had been a Guide as a girl and she'd always longed to start a company. Ruth Du Feu, who's now Mrs Le Boutillier, and I were founder members of the Girls' Collegiate Nineteenth Company. It went on from then until the school closed. I loved it! I had to leave the Guides when I left school at fifteen and a half. I had to, I didn't have the time once I'd started work on the farm.

I'd wanted to be a music teacher and a nurse, I thought I could combine the two, eventually becoming a doctor, of course. I had big ideas! I was very ambitious. Even then I had a finger in every pie! But my father was quite right when he said,

"I'll continue to pay for you to learn music with Leonard Herivel but what's the point of me paying for you to become a music teacher, when by twenty you'll be married!"

I kept on with the St. John Ambulance, which I'd also been introduced to whilst at the Collegiate, for a little while and carried on independently with my music, though not with Leonard Herivel. I couldn't become a nurse either, and at the time I did regret it, but still there were other compensations. I loved the outdoor life, I could drive a tractor before I could bake a cake, much to my mother's horror! We worked hard. The côtils at Rozel, with the tomatoes and potatoes, were very hard work. As I was growing up I was expected to help in the house with the youngsters and milk the cows. The milking was done by hand then. Dad and Mum weren't too hard on us, unlike some parents who got their children up at some unearthly hour. Obviously at the weekend it was different, as when we left school, we worked full time.

Carmel Farm had a delightful house, snuggled into the hillside. I shared my bedroom with Maureen. It was great fun, coming in late at night and sneaking up the stairs. Once we were late coming in and Dad and Mum had already gone to bed. We'd left the window unlatched so we went up the stairs, knowing exactly where to avoid the creaking stair, but Dad suddenly heard our bedroom door and came to investigate. We shot into bed fully dressed!

We had a twin-seated toilet in the garden, by the fig tree, which we called the 'double-decker'. It was a very happy childhood, a very happy background. Mum kept us all together and always urged Dad on the right side if we wanted something. We were very close even though the three younger ones were much younger than us. Obviously we had our little moments, as every family does, but our Mum was a young thinking person, the family's driving force, and a very loving mum. I still miss her terribly.

My father was a true Jerseyman, his bark was worse than his bite. He was more a grower than a cattleman. We kept a few cows of course, chickens and a few pigs but we relied on the early potatoes and tomatoes.

I have always loved singing, anything to do with music. I've done quite a lot of singing, soloist and choir work. When I was sixteen I joined the Young Farmers' Club and, of course, was involved with the concerts. I made a lot of 'lifetime friendships' whilst in the Young Farmers' – in fact Les and I are part of four couples who are still firm friends from those early days, Len and Ruth Picot, Denis and Eileen Renouf and Arthur and Mollie Querée. We get together often for dinner and sometimes holiday together.

The club took up a lot of my time for I was very much involved. I became treasurer eventually and took part in the shows, debates, all sorts of things. There was a show every year. Singing was my main thing, until I took over the piano. We used to go around all the Parish Halls with the concerts. It was a full time interest until we became twenty-five years old, when you had to leave. Les was Vice President when we got married, and by the time we left we had two children. It was great fun.

It was through the Young Farmers' Club that Les and I met. As Les told you he came down to Carmel on spec and invited me to the Bouley Bay Hill Climb on the Easter Monday. I went on a visit to Denmark on an exchange visit with the club. Les couldn't come because he had the farm to look after and, rather naughtily, he proposed to me the night before I left, asking Len Picot to keep an eye on me while we were away!

On the way to the airport I told my dad that Les was going to call and ask if we could get married.

"What?!" he shouted.

I was only nineteen and the first born of his five daughters. Even though he didn't say so to us, he told everyone else that he wouldn't change his five girls for five boys, which was rather nice. I collected bits and pieces towards our home for my bottom drawer and we got engaged on Les's birthday in February and married in the November. There was no reason for us to wait, even though I'm sure people counted on their fingers at the time! Les's widowed mother was quite elderly and had already moved into the dower cottage.

We married at eleven o'clock on November 15th, 1950, at Trinity Church. We chose that time of the year so that we could both be finished with our farm work. There were no such things as facials and hairdos for brides then. I did my own hair and it was the tin bath in front of the fire! At nine o'clock it poured, and I mean poured, with rain. My mother was frantically organising umbrellas! I had a lovely white dress, and Juliet cap, made by Madame Blondeau who lived in New Street, by St. Thomas's Church. She was excellent with her needle. It was a layered dress with all

We too Remember When...

Mazel and Les on their wedding day.

seed pearls around. It was beautiful. Well, half past ten came and the sun came out. When we were ready my father and I waited for the taxi, which was late. A next door neighbour, who had a motor bike and side-car came, ready to drive me to the church in case the car didn't arrive! Unknown to us a friend and neighbour of Les's was waiting down at Rozel to give us a shot-gun send off but they shot the telephone wires down! So we were a bit late arriving.

Arthur Querée, the ex-Constable of St. Ouen, was our best man and two of my sisters, and Les's sister, were bridesmaids. Our reception was at the Ritz Hotel. The Ritz Hotel in Colomberie isn't there any more but it was lovely. Our reception was held in a lovely big room and we had a pianist playing romantic music, especially as I love piano music; it really was lovely! It was very difficult to keep the numbers down because in those days you used to invite distant relations, great uncles and aunts, and all the elderly relatives. We had a three-tiered wedding cake made by Mr De La Haye at Haut Croix Stores, where he had his bakehouse. Afterwards we caught the five o'clock plane to Southampton.

∾

I met my husband at All Saints Church. He was in the choir and also in charge of organising the camping for visiting scout groups. All Saints used to hold a Whist Drive once a week, above the Smiths Mineral Water in Cannon Street, and that's where we actually met.

My sister and I had a double wedding, early in the morning. We didn't have far to go from our home at Westmount. There were no cars then but couples would often walk from their individual homes to the church and back, without hiring a carriage. We wore ordinary dresses, no bridesmaids. Getting married at that time in the morning, with them having to get ready to catch the boat, well, we wouldn't have dressed up all in white! Besides afterwards my sister and her husband went to catch the boat to St. Malo. They were travelling through France to Belgium for their honeymoon.

We were married at St. Paul's. We could have had the service at All Saints but Dick, my brother-in-law, was involved at St. Paul's so we said we'd get married there as well. I can't remember the minister's name, it's too long ago.

Alicia Priddy

My wife Dill and I knew each other from kids. Our early life centred on the swimming pool at Havre Des Pas. I was very friendly with Robert Bryant, who became a chemist, and my mother used to go down to the pool with old Mrs McCready and they used to be down there, doing their knitting, and we'd go and join them after school. I knew Dill then, my brothers knew her brothers, but I think she thought us horrible little boys at that time.

Then we had nothing to do with one another until after the Occupation when I met her at a party. She was with Ruth Norman and some others, and she got rid of her boyfriend, and I got rid of my girlfriend, and we went out together. We got married and went to live in Guernsey when I got demobbed.

We've celebrated our Golden Wedding. Incredible how time has gone by. Here we are with four kids and twelve grandchildren!

Reverend Geoffrey Baker

I met my husband at one of the Agriculture Shows at Springfield. He'd been transferred to a bank over here. We always dressed up to go to the shows and I remember I was wearing a large picture hat of red and white straw, a red *crêpe de chine* suit with tassels going down of white, a pair of red and white shoes that I'd bought for 4s.11d in London and gloves with red and white in them. And here I was sitting next to this fellow with curly hair, dressed in a blazer and grey flannels, with an open neck shirt! Oh! I was disgusted!

Afterwards we went to have a meal out somewhere so it was dark

We too Remember When...

coming back and I'd happened to say I didn't like walking up the long drive to our house because of frogs. (I'd walked on a frog once and I'd always remembered it!) Well, this curly haired chap said, "I'll walk up with you," and I thought 'hmmmm!'

It was straight after that I went to London and when I came back I went to mum and I said, "You won't believe it but the first chap I met was that curly-haired one!"

And it developed from that! He invited me out for a walk one Sunday. I was dressed up in a fur coat I remember and once again he had an open necked shirt on.

"Excuse me," he said, "can you just wait two minutes. I won't be long!" and he went back to his digs and put on a suit! I thought that was lovely, don't you think so too? We joked about that often! He used to say, 'Can you imagine coming from London to a little place like Jersey and going to a country fair all dressed up?!' But of course we Jersey took dressing up for granted! We were married at St. Paul's in New Street, in 1937.

Kay Wills

Senator Frank Walker was born in 1943...

I was the only surviving, natural, child of my parents. They had a series of tragedies. The worst one was when one of their sons, who I never knew because he died before I was born, died at the age of five. I don't think my father ever recovered from that, not ever I don't think. They also had other babies who were stillborn or lived a couple of hours. They had a terrible time. They were told they shouldn't have any more children and, against medical advice, they had me. I wasn't very strong either so they were very protective.

When I was nearly four they adopted my sister Anne. As we grew up she and I didn't get on at all, not at all, but now we get on so well. We lived between Le Hocq and Green Island and on one side of us, there were three houses in a row. We had the Wagstaff family who were my cousins, and on the other side we had the Scriven family, who were also my cousins. So we had this expanded family unit. There were little strips of land on the beach side of the road in front of our properties so we had direct access to the beach and, because it's very difficult for the general public to get to, it was almost like having our own private beach. What a

Frank as a boy

way to be brought up. It was fantastic!

I started off at Landsdown Preparatory in Dicq Road. It was a super school. We had a real traditional education without any frills at all. I remember if you spoke in class or committed a minor offence you got a whack over the knuckles with a ruler and, of course, you're not allowed to do that anymore. But it didn't do us any harm.

The Bailiff, Philip Bailhache, was there. I lived in terror of him. Mind you, I was a, well, a modern day term would be... a wimp. I was very frail. I had trouble with my eyes when I was a young kid, a tremendous problem, and that prevented me from doing all sorts of things. So it was very easy for boys to push me around.

I don't know when Landsdown closed but it's been gone a long time. I was there for about two years and then I went to Prep. I had a hard time initially at Prep, again because of my eyes. My parents did everything to cure the problem but nothing much worked. The eye specialist said that I'd grow out of it and of course I did.

By the time I came to leave the Prep at the age of eleven I was beginning to get a bit more adventurous and a bit more normal. I got an Open Scholarship to Victoria College, at a time when they were not given out too frequently, and everyone was very pleased. However, at about fourteen, my interest in education just nosedived. I had discovered girls! I wasn't remotely interested in education, not remotely. In fact it got so serious that the then Director of Education, Mr Wimberly, wrote to my father with my school report – which came in the middle of the summer holidays – saying that if I didn't pull my socks up they'd take my scholarship away from me. As you can imagine my father wasn't too pleased! That was a fairly traumatic summer holiday.

My parents were very possessive and, not surprisingly, they worried like crazy about me which caused problems when I was a teenager. It was fine up to then because with my eye problems I had been weedy but when this passed, and I became a normal teenager, obviously I wanted to do all the things normal teenagers do. They were very tough on me with curfews in the evening. I was always having to get back in an hour or so before most of my friends or cousins and of course that was mortifying to a teenager. I rebelled. We had a pretty uneasy time for two or three years.

I took eight 'O' Levels and only got three, and of course that was very bad too. So instead of going up to the Sixth Form with my group I stayed in Upper Fifth for another year and retook my 'O' Levels and got six, including the three that I got before. Then I left school. I didn't bother with 'A' Levels at all. My parents gave up. They realised that I wasn't going to continue.

So I joined the *Evening Post*. I didn't have much option, well, I say I didn't have any option but nobody forced me to go. I couldn't think of anything else to do really. I had no ambition, absolutely no ambition at all. It was clearly, in all sorts of ways, the best thing I could possibly have done because I was euphemistically called a 'Management Trainee'. They'd never had a Management Trainee in the *Evening Post* before, didn't really know what to do with me, so I started off in the Pressroom.

I did three years in the Pressroom and that was really hard work. It toughened me up physically and mentally because I had to carry heavy stuff around, very frequently, throughout every day. The press plates themselves were very big, heavy, lead-based plates in those days and I frequently carried two at a time, so that really built me up. The men were tough on me too, as they needed to be. They didn't show me any favours or give me any privileges at all. I was pushed around and made to do all the dirty jobs, all the difficult jobs, exactly as it should have been.

Then I had three glorious years of working in the Type Setting, the 'Composing Room' as it was called, which I absolutely adored. We used to start work at eight, get on with the job, and finish by four. There was never any work to take home and no responsibilities at all. So you'd leave at four and, in summer particularly, that was fantastic. You'd just get on and enjoy life. It was wonderful. I really did enjoy that very much. I ended up by completing the National Graphical Association, as it then was, Apprenticeship – so I'm a fully-fledged Printer!

After that they put me down into the front office, which you remember was on the corner of Bath Street and Charles Street. We just served the public there. They came in to pay their accounts, and we used to sell newspapers in those days too. There used to be a queue outside the door, waiting for the paper, do you remember? It was really a part of town life in those days. Very much so. Crowds would wait outside for the election and the Muratti results. But of course it's all so different today, with radio and T.V.

That was a good time for me as well because that was the first time I met the public, as it were, in the professional sense. Then one day Eric Le Cornu, who was the advertisement manager (in those days Eric used to wait for advertisements to come in. Nobody used to go out to sell as they do today) decided that he wanted to go out to sell a special feature on the summer ball and flower festival. He couldn't do it so he asked me to go and try. Well, of course I'd never sold any advertisements to anybody, but I went out. I still remember the first advertisement I ever sold to anyone. It was to Bertha De La Taste, the florist. I remember walking out of her shop on cloud nine. I'd succeeded! I'd made the company some money! It went on from there with that particular feature being very successful.

They put me back into the front office again but I didn't want to stay there then. I'd tasted going out to sell advertising and found that this was what I wanted to do. So I made a real nuisance of myself with my uncles Arthur Harrison and Jim Scriven, who were running the business then, and eventually they appointed me Sales Rep, which is what I wanted. I enjoyed that. That was the time I really found myself. That was my niche.

We used to have an office on the third floor and one day Eric was walking down the stairs and he met Jim Scriven coming up. They had a slight altercation and Eric walked out of the front door and never came back! So they had nobody then to run the Advertising Department and the only one with any experience at all was myself. They appointed me Advertising Manager, I was only... how old was I?... twenty-five I suppose, and they gave me a wage increase of ten shillings a week! An amazing rise for going from representative to manager, but then money wasn't that important to me. I had enough to spend on myself.

We got in another advertisement representative, then another one, and then we introduced artists for the first time, so we had some creativity coming into the ads for the first time ever. We ended up with a team of five. Mary Gaiger (she's still at the *Evening Post*, and is now Sales Director), Al Thomas, a brilliant artist, Peter Tabb, who's got his own company and another young artist called Barry Bromley, who subsequently left to go to New Zealand where he has done very well indeed. We were happy. The

We too Remember When...

five of us got on ever so well, socialising as well as working together. The advertising figures went up. It was an exciting time, breaking new ground, trying new things. We were living a tremendous life, it was really good fun.

Then I did the same thing as Eric. I had a bit of a debate with Jim Scriven and I resigned and a few months later set up my own advertising agency, Walkers Associates. Mary and Barry came to join me so we were the founding directors. We started off actually working from Barry's parents' house. Mary and I were manning the telephones in the lounge and Barry was producing the artwork in his bedroom. It was a bit scary because there was the risk, but I've never been afraid of risk – ever. At least I wasn't then. I am probably just a bit more so now. Then there was the brashness of youth.

We ran Walkers Associates for four years, very successfully, and again tremendous fun. Then I came back from a skiing holiday with my, then, wife and my mother told me that the family had decided, for reasons that I've never fully understood, that the *Evening Post* was going to be sold.

I didn't want it to be sold out of Jersey, or out of the family, so I went around knocking on the doors of several banks and got laughed out of most of them. I was twenty-nine, no real business experience, nothing to suggest that I could run a newspaper or certainly one the size of the *Evening Post*. Eventually thanks to Peter Giffard, the Advocate, and Don Nicolle who was then Manager of the Midland Bank in Hill Street, I got backing from the Midland and made an offer for the company. Sadly my uncle Arthur, who held one third of the shares, declined my offer but I ended up, either by buying or with the support of the rest of the company, taking over the business. So at the age of twenty-nine, in 1973, I was Managing Director of the *Jersey Evening Post*. It was a dream come true.

If somebody had asked me, a number of years prior to that time, "What would be your ideal job?" I would have said just that.

> **Reverend Geoffrey Baker** *was born in 1926, in a little house called Bizerta, in Green Street...*

I was the youngest of four children. Nance, Peter and Arthur were born close together and it was seven years before I came along. I must have been a mistake I'm sure! My brother Peter always said he remembered my father coming down the stairs and saying, "It's another little bugger!" but what he had said was, "It's another little brother!"

I remember when I was about nine or ten my parents must have fallen out with the vicar of St. Marks for we were marched off, with stiff collars and a cough sweet in our mouths, to St. James. It's strange to think that years later I was to become Vicar of the church my parents walked me away from!

We went to Church as a duty. I can remember Peter and Arthur never wanting to go and Peter hiding out the back. I remember him throwing stones and breaking the window of the people next door and our parents saying, "You must go next door and apologise!" and he ran, knocked on the door, said "Sorry!" and ran back again. And he ended up a Jurat!

We moved around quite a bit when I was younger, for from Green Street we moved to St Mark's Road, and from there back to Brockenhurst in Green Street, by which time I was at the Prep. Then just before the Occupation we moved again, this time up to a grand house at Bellozanne. My Dad was quite a modest fellow. He never thought he could afford something like that until a relation told him that he could do better than the house in Green Street.

I didn't get ordained until we had our four kids. I was in my thirties by then. I nearly went mad trying to make up my mind whether I should or not for though I had a love/hate thing with the Church, I'd always been drawn to it. A lot of me thought it was more interesting than making money in the shop. Then when Dad died and left a bit of money it enabled me to manage whilst I was away at theological college. Dill stayed in Guernsey with the children and when the Bishop said they needed a Curate at St. Marks we came back to Jersey. The Vicar then was Reverend Godfrey and when he decided to retire they pulled me up one instead of taking on a new vicar. So I stayed at St. Marks.

I enjoyed that. It was great, a really thriving church. When we first returned to Jersey we rented a house at the bottom of St. Saviour's Hill called Waverly Lodge, but when I was made Vicar they pulled down the

We too Remember When...

old vicarage and rebuilt the new one and we lived there. It was really busy, hectic. A great ten or twelve years.

From then I've done more individual, pastoral, things. I don't regret my life at all. I've had a much more interesting life than if I'd stayed in the business, though I sometimes wonder if there are many people who have been in as many Jersey houses as I have!

❧

Sir Philip Bailhache, *Bailiff of Jersey, was born at a little Nursing Home, Greenwood, which was on the coast road in St. Clement, in 1946...*

I was the eldest of four children. I have two sisters and one brother. Both sisters now live in England and my brother is in practice at the bar in Jersey.

My mother used to have French Au Pair girls who came over to learn English, besides helping in the house but, when we were growing up, we had to do the ordinary family tasks that one used to do. I'm not sure that I was a particularly nice elder brother to my sisters. I used to pay very small amounts of money to the elder one, Val, who was two years younger than me, to be my slave and carry out various menial tasks! She was an extremely loving and adorable small sister.

My parents were fairly strict, I think. There would certainly have been severe consequences if I had done anything which I had been forbidden to do. They were reasonable but they were strict in the sense that they had expectations and all their children were required to meet those expectations. We went to St. Clement's Church, as a family. I remember Mr Hornby was the Rector at the time.

My first school was Landsdown Pre-Preparatory School which was a double-roomed school run by two splendid ladies, one of them was a Mrs Noel and the other was called Miss Deacon. They ran this small school just off Dicq Road for boys and for girls. One of my fellow pupils at that time was John Averty, now the Managing Director of the Guiton Group. It was an extremely good little school, where I suppose they took children between the ages of four and six or seven and taught us all the basics. I started learning French at five or six. I enjoyed languages and still do.

One of the things I remember, which would not be appropriate

Sir Philip (upper left) as a boy with his family.

nowadays, is that Mrs Noel used to divide up the children into boys and girls for playtime. The girls used to be required to stand in the upper part of the playground and the boys were relegated to the lower part where they could run around and be noisy, hit each other and play football. The poor little girls were required to behave themselves!

I went from that school to St. Michaels and stayed there until thirteen when I went away to school in England. I suppose I did all the usual things that small boys did. I used to swim and potter about on the beach.

I was a contemporary of Doug Le Masurier, who now runs the Oyster and Mussel Farm at La Rocque, and of Mike Taylor who is now a professional fisherman and Chairman of the Fishermen's Association. We used to go on the beach quite regularly and go fishing off the rocks for little things which, I think, were called *cabots*. We used to have a little hook on the end of a piece of string, with some bait in the form of a limpet, and catch these poor miserable little fish and take them back home. I'm not sure if they were given to the cat or just allowed to die!

I suppose a lot of my childhood, because I later went to England, was spent away from the island. School holidays were relatively short. There were no half term periods as there are now. It was the extended periods of the summer holidays, the most time I spent on the island after the age of thirteen, that I remember most. There was a lot of going to the beach, I remember, a lot of going to St. Ouen's and surfing off the beach there.

We too Remember When...

In my teens I started playing golf. My father was, is, a keen and good golfer and we used to play together. We had a lot of fun doing that. Yes, I had a very happy and contented childhood, which laid some good foundations.

How did I feel about going away to school? Well, St. Michael's primes you for going away and I had boarded there for a term or two before actually leaving. I was obviously a bit unhappy during the first few weeks that I was away but I soon got used to that. I enjoyed playing football and other sports and they were very important at boarding schools in those days. So I settled down very quickly and started to enjoy myself.

I left there to go to Pembroke College, Oxford, when I was eighteen. I suppose I had thought that I would become a lawyer at a fairly early age, although it was not something that I can really remember making a specific decision about. It seemed to happen almost by accident, because when I went to University I had to decide what I was going to study. The choice lay between languages and something completely different so I decided to read law. Then I suppose my career path was set. I spent three years at Pembroke before going to read for the Bar in London. It was immediately after I qualified, more or less, that I came back to Jersey. That was 1968.

At the beginning I had no intention of coming back to Jersey. I remember, just after I'd qualified at the English Bar, applying for a job with the United Nations, in the International Labour Office. I wasn't successful, I think they wanted somebody with more experience, so for family reasons I then decided I should come back to Jersey. My father was getting on and I think he wanted to hand over the family practice, at 14, Hill Street, to one of his sons if he could. So I came back, qualified at the Jersey Bar, and practiced in the family firm for five or six years before becoming Solicitor General.

Certainly the legal profession at that time was very much smaller than it is now and practising law was rather different too. Our firm was a family business with very much a local clientèle whom we knew personally. Now the clientèle is so vast. Jersey was not as busy then. It was, I suppose, a time when the island had not really become a financial centre though it was moving in that direction.

Daff Noël

I didn't go to school until I was seven. I went on the back of my brother Arthur's bike to the Prep. Dear old Miss Aubrey taught me to read. I've loved her ever since. Then they had a Miss Bunnett, I think she was called, as a Headmistress and the Headmaster was Mr Hopewell.

I was the first boy to get the cane at the Prep. I was just showing off to the rest of the class, pretending to stick a pen into the backside of a teacher who was writing on the blackboard and he stepped back into the pen. Aaah! Off I went for the cane!

I'd hate my children to be like that with me, but I was so wanting my parents to think I was a good little boy that I never told them, until it crept out. Some aunt, who had a boy at the College said, "Did you know that Geoffrey had the cane?" They were very sweet and upset that I hadn't told them.

I hated going to school. I think in those days people were much more nervous of starting school, there was no pre-prep or nursery attachments to schools then. I don't really think kids should go to school so early. I think parents are too keen to get rid of them myself. All this about you getting on better in later life if you go to school at three years is rubbish. I think kids would rather have less money and more home life.

I can remember screaming my head off at going to the dentist, being terrified and loathing having my hair cut. I must have been a nervous child. My parents used to let me go off to the pictures with Robert Bryant and, though the films were nothing like you would see at the cinema now, something would stick in my mind so that when I went to bed I would think someone was trying to get in the window! I lived in my own little world. I was a loner with one or two special friends. Even now I've never been one of the 'Old Boys' or gone to reunions or anything like that. I can't bear going around with groups.

I enjoyed going to Victoria College, and being in the same form as Tim Voisin (I remember his parents being killed in that air crash), but I have to say that when my mother got me to England and the Grammar School in Dorset, they were so caring, and I got on so well, that I tend to think I did better than if I had stayed at the College. I went into university from there before being called up within a few months and, joining the Intelligence Corps, went on out to the Far East.

Reverend Geoffrey Baker

We too Remember When...

At the end of our garden was a wall of the school in New St. John's Road that was run by Miss Biddle. It was a mixed school so, until I was about six or seven, I went there. Only one room it was, with boys and girls sitting around. Do you know a man came to read my meter years ago and he said,

"I know you don't I?" and I said,

"Yes, you do! We went to that little school together!"

Imagine! We still remembered one another!

But one day my father said,

"She's never going to learn anything there!"

So I went to Brighton Road. Miss Bowes was the Headmistress. She was very tough, eh. We had one teacher, who couldn't control, and we were having this lesson this day and some girls were playing up - you always get them, eh. Well, that was it. She started crying and she rushed out of the room and went to fetch Miss Bowers. She came in – oh! my God, one look! She banged on her desk and said,

"I'll take them for this lesson from now on!"

I was never caned but I did get a clip around the head from Miss Richard. French she was. She was a bit of a battle axe, so was Miss Mauger. But there was Miss Machon, she was lovely, very tall – Miss Le Riche, do you remember her? Ahh! She was lovely.

It was a good school. 3 R's, spelling every day, you were *taught* lessons you know. But if you were naughty you were sent to stand outside of the class, in the hall, and Miss Bowers had her desk out there. Well! You couldn't help but be seen, eh?!

Iris de la Mare née Morris

...which meant you 'couldn't help' but get the cane! As I remember too well!

Daff Noël

My family originally came to Jersey in 1920, when I was twelve, and I finished my education at the Ladies' College. Having attended a good school in England and passing all the exams, it wasn't necessary for me to sit an entrance exam. The papers were simply exchanged between the schools. I liked it at the Ladies' College. Miss d'Hautrée was the headmistress at the time. We learnt Latin, though I don't remember any now. It's known as the Girls' College now. Why they had to change the name I don't know. It's stupid isn't it? Why alter the name? There's no difference between a lady and a girl. To many locals today it is still referred to as the Ladies' College. I think it's a shame they moved the girls to Mont Millais. The old building in Rouge Bouillon was such an elegant building.

Alicia Priddy

I had started off school at St. Aloysious's School, Berry House, in Val Plaisant. Do you remember it? It was next to St. Thomas's Church, that little building there, remember? Well, that was part of the Beeches, De La Salle College. There were two brothers, Brother James and Brother Peter, running it. We were there for about eighteen months to two years I think, before we all moved up to the main school on Wellington Road. I was at the Beeches until 1930 when I was fourteen. Dad was starting up this new shop, he wanted some help, I was keen, so he asked me to go and help him. He gave the school notice that I was leaving and I went into the shop.

Henry (Pat) Letto

I went to school at Pontac, a very small school, just near the Bon Air Hotel. The school was run by Miss Ahier, a mixed school it was. I suppose there were about thirty of us. I left when I was about fourteen to go into hairdressing. My sister had private teaching at home because she wasn't in very good health. How my parents afforded it I don't know because we weren't very well off. My two brothers went to the Jersey Modern School. That started off in Colomberie before moving to La Coie Hall in Springfield Road (if you remember, it later became a hotel). Mr Job was a master when my brothers were there. I'll always remember that. He was a young man then of course and it was long before he took up the Headship at St. George's.

Joan Letto

My first school was at Madame Berthe, which was further up St. Saviour's Road, on the right-hand side. It only had about two classrooms. 2s.6d a week it was. Dad had to pay. That's all the money he could afford. I went on to New Street school and stayed there until I left at fourteen. Max Le Feuvre was the Headmaster. He was quite strict. I had the cane – for talking. They were hard on you then.

John Blampied

We too Remember When...

I went to the F.C.J. briefly. I remember taking the number 11 bus to the top of Jubilee Hill – walking through the town – the horrible smell of burnt scrambled eggs coming from the brewery! Yes! I thought the hops smelt just like burnt scrambled eggs! But I hated the travel, the buses in the winter, so I was sent to boarding school, in Guernsey.

We flew on one of the little Rapides. Did you ever travel on them? There were five or six of us little girls who went to the Convent in Guernsey and we sat behind the pilot with a bag of barley sugars. I loved the school in Guernsey. It was especially nice because my friends and I went together.

Lady Anne Wilkes

Do you remember when there was a school on the St. Paul's Centre site; first New Street, then briefly St. Helier Boys' School? **Peter Le Masurier** *recalls memories of his secondary education at the latter...*

Having finished with my Primary School education at St. Clement I started at St. Helier Boys' School in September 1957. We had to assemble at La Motte Street School that first morning, before we all walked down to New Street and were told what class we would be in. We had a large playground and a tuck shop where you could obtain crisps, ice-cream and fizzy pop. During our mid-day lunch break I would sometimes walk down to Gaudins and wait to see my Dad come past on his bicycle. He was always delighted to see me and spend a few minutes chatting. (Poor Dad, he only had one hour for lunch but cycled from the J.M.T. workshops on the Esplanade to Samarès Lane, where we lived.)

Because we had no gym facilities at New Street School we had to walk down to Seaton Place (what is now the Seaton Youth Centre) on certain days. Mr Ken Webb was the instructor and was quite strict. I could never get over that vaulting horse!

An incident that I shall never forget took place one day in February. The cold winter day started off as normal, but by about twelve noon it had gone completely dark. Some of the boys were saying the end of the world had come. I was quite frightened and when some lad said we could all go home (unofficially) we all went, only to get the wrath of Miss Gough's tongue the next day!

"Who gave you permission to go? Come on, own up!"

Peter as a boy.

What happened was that there had been a large build up of snow clouds which had made it go like night-time. It was strange to see the lights on in the T.S.B. Bank at noon!

I also remember a little shop in New Street called Tally's where I used to purchase coloured matches for November 5th. The other shop we used to go to was Winnie's, on the corner of Dumaresq Street (now Morgan Grenville). She sold sweets, comics and second-hand books.

One of the highlights of New Street School was an educational visit to the Val de la Mare dam, which was under construction. We went by coach and received a packed lunch. The teachers told us to bring a camera, if we had one, but the only camera we had at home was a box camera of my Dad's. I felt too embarrassed to take it but quite a few of the boys brought these cameras along. So I missed out on getting any pictures of the dam being built!

I can't remember at what stage we transferred to La Motte Street but I remember we had a hall where we had assembly and sang the school hymn, which went something like this...

*Now as I start upon my chosen way,
in all I do, my thoughts, my work, my play,
help me to keep my honour shining bright.
To be the best, the very best that I can be.*

There may have been another verse but I cannot remember it.

We had a Science Room, a Woodwork Room, and Metalwork Room. I enjoyed Science and won a prize for it. (I find it quite strange going back to the building today – it's now the State's Greffe Print Section – and remembering the Science Room, which is now the paper store. You can even see where the drinking fountain used to be in the playground!)

I was in Mr Harris's class which was on the first floor and, facing you as you came out of the class was a large mural, on the wall, of St. Helier being executed with two hatchets, which in those days was the school's

We too Remember When...

blazer and cap badge. Mr Harris was a wonderful teacher. He was into art and craft but took many subjects. He got some of us to record a play using sound effects. I was the narrator. I remember hearing my voice in 'Crooks & Cushions' by Agnes Booth. It was good fun... but we had to do it *after* school!

Once or twice a year we had a cross-country run. It started from the F.B. Fields, going across the Golf Course, jumping the small brook and on to La Blinerie Lane, down Samarès Lane, onto the Coast Road to run as far as Grève D'Azette then back along the Inner Road to the F.B. Fields. The last ones back (the fatties!) had to do one circuit of the F.B. Fields. It was great running down Samarès Lane because my Mother would wait by the gate of our little cottage and give me a drink and a bar of chocolate as I passed by... to keep me going.

By the November/December of 1960 all the finishing touches were being made to the 'New St. Helier Boys' School' on St. Saviour's Hill. All the teachers were as excited as we pupils about the move and kept us informed. The removal date was given for what was to be the school's final home.

"We need volunteers to help move some of the equipment like books etc.," said one of the teachers.

"I will sir!" chorused quite a few of the lads.

Unfortunately it had to be done *during* the Christmas school holidays! And so came that morning in January 1961 when we all lined up in the playground, facing the large hall and front door of the new school. Monitors and Prefects helped those who did not know where to line up, for don't forget it was all new and strange to quite a lot of the lads. Only those who had volunteered to help with the move had had a preview of what was to come. Line by line we made our way into the brand new hall with its highly polished floor, its large stage with spotlights and two colour ceiling of blue and white panels, and that lovely smell of fresh paint!

After Mr A.H. Downer had welcomed us and laid down a few rules we made our way up the stairs to our brand new classrooms. My classroom was overlooking Government House and we could see the time on the clock on St. Saviour's Church. On the south side of the school we could see the Jesuit Priests walking around the grounds of Highlands (now Highlands College) with their Bibles. At the west end of the school you could see the summer house on the corner of Westmount (demolished a few years ago).

Some areas were out of bounds and a few of us got into trouble for venturing too far. We had a brand new gym with showers adjoining and a small swimming pool. The playing fields were not yet completed and on that first day I remember the bulldozer levelling out the earth (that same bulldozer is now in the Steam Museum). The Science Block was not yet built so we still had to return to La Motte Street on some days.

Unfortunately, whilst at the new school, I got on the wrong side of Mr Downer. In those days I had to catch two buses, one from the top of Samarès Lane to Snow Hill Bus Station, then another as far as St. Saviour's Church but this did not get to the school until 9.05 a.m. I was summoned to his study to explain why I was five minutes late every day. He did not accept my explanation (you had no say in those days) and wrote to my Mum saying I was "insolent and truculent". (I think I'd told him I was not going to walk from Snow Hill to school but of course I ended up doing just that!)

My time at the New St. Helier Boys' School was short lived for in those days you could leave at fifteen. The day came when we had to talk to the teachers about what we were going to do. "I want to join the Army sir," said one lad.

"And me!" said another.

"I want to be a butcher sir," somebody else said.

"And what about you Le Masurier?"

"I want to be a printer sir." (My dad had always told me it was a good job.)

"My uncle was a compositor," said Mr Pyman.

"What is that sir?"

"A compositor puts words together for printing," he explained.

So in May 1961, five months after the school opened its doors I started a six year apprenticeship at Bigwoods, Wesley Street... but that's another story.

As I look back on my schooldays I do think they were the best years of my life but you do not realise it at the time. I had many wonderful school friends, some of them have sadly died, but many are still here and when we see each other we talk about those wonderful days.

I am so glad to have been part of that wonderful experience of moving into class 4B, in Millais House, of a brand new school, albeit 38 years ago.

We too Remember When...

> **Mr Leo Harris**, the class teacher mentioned in Peter's recollections, remembers too...

I had been invited by the newly appointed headmaster, Arthur Downer, to join him on the staff of a new educational project for Jersey, the beginning of St. Helier Boys' school. It was early in 1952 and I had known Arthur Downer for a little over a year as a student teacher on 'school practice' at First Tower School, of which he was then the Head. The letter of appointment came as a complete surprise when I received it at College in Twickenham. Finding a job was very difficult for a newly fledged teacher at that time and I was making overtures to the Royal Navy for a commission in the Instructor Branch.

I had a great liking for teaching and had returned to First Tower School, after completing my school practice, when I came back to Jersey for the summer. It was June and the schools were still at work for another month. My offer of unpaid assistance had been accepted but, unknown to me, Arthur had arranged that I should be paid and at the end of term he surprised me by giving me a pay cheque for £28.

You must not imagine for a moment that teaching in Jersey, in an elementary school as they were then called, was other than the most pleasant of occupations. The schools were beautifully maintained by the Education Office, working out of Library Place, and had a Victorian, or, at least Edwardian, style to them. The buildings were kept in pristine condition from day to day by selfless caretakers and their families. They worked as a team – father, mother and the children. In winter, generous coal fires glowed in the classroom and in spring, light and airy corridors were fresh with cool air and the murmurs of well disciplined children at work. It was totally delightful. I may add that the bane of all teachers, the electronic photocopier, had not even been thought of, not even a twinkle in a young scientist's eye. Copying at that time was on the primitive 'Jellygraph' which operated, as its name implies, in a foolscap size tray of purple jelly from which individual copies could be retrieved from an equally messy 'master'. Oh yes, the Gestetner was to be found in the Head's study covered, as ever, in black printing ink and surrounded by rejected paper jams.

It was into this lovely time warp that I was to be inducted. The first staff meeting was to be held in the afternoon of a July day in 1952 at New Street School. I arrived on my motorbike and parked in the school yard, now St. Paul's Gate in Dumaresq Street. Surrounded by fading white-painted sets of cricket stumps painted directly onto the high cement faced walls, I saw a truly Victorian building with at least three granite entrances each one announcing its graven intention to admit only BOYS, GIRLS or INFANTS. I chose INFANTS and found myself in a strange classroom in which one face of the step pyramid climbed steadily backwards, and ever upwards, until it finally ended, not against an azure sky, but against a church window. Each step had its row of oak and cast iron pupils' desks with clanging folding seats, and lids which hinged open to reveal the ink graffiti of the earlier part of the twentieth century, and some a little earlier than that. An odour of sandwiches and old, cheap paper wafted upwards from these Pandora boxes, while old prints and well worn maps of the world, covered with faded pink patches, curled quietly on the wall as if in dumb acceptance that their time had come. Nearby, on the wall, was a rack so arranged that it held perhaps six or eight canes in order of thickness to suit the punishment to the crime.

The new staff were introduced to each other and I cannot help but reflect on how very few of those fine professional men and women are left today. May I just mention one or two? Mrs Parkes. She fitted the Victorian image to a tee and, indeed, had been teaching at New Street School for many years under the Headship of Max Le Feuvre, himself a character in his time. Mrs Parkes was in appearance a slight, rather 'fey' character with wisps of auburn and greying hair. I imagine she may have been in her late fifties but to me, at twenty-one going on twenty-two, she seemed of great age and straight out of Dickens and possibly 'Great Expectations'. She spoke beautifully in a well-modulated voice. I learned to recognise that voice as its tones drifted across a corridor and into my Art Room. She commanded her 'boys' with breathtaking discipline and supreme authority born of years of experience of just such boys. She knew their parents, their aunties, uncles, their grandparents and other family details over which many of her 'charges' would gladly have drawn a veil. But I was stunned by her ability to mesmerise her class by reading to them. I recall very clearly one day when I came across her reading from *Shadow the Sheep-dog*. I swear that most of the boys were crying as they listened to her expressing every emotion from the nineteenth century novel.

Arthur Downer I knew well, his two deputies were very different from one another. Jack Clark was a Londoner. He had come to Jersey just after the war ended and had been teaching at La Motte Street School before

Above: The staff of St. Helier's Boys' School (New Street) about 1954.
Back row, left to right: Miss Gough, Jack Godeaux, Leo Harris, Michael Hubbard.
Front row, left to right: Gerry Woodsford, Edwin Le Marquand, Jack Clark, Des Danican, Derek Le Maistre.

Below: The second year form, with 'Sir' centre, taken in the school playground, New Street, about 1954/5.

joining the staff of St. Helier Boys' School. Likeable and clever with a great sense of humour, Jack loved cricket and indoctrinated any number of boys into its mysteries. He was kind and most often gentle with his charges but had a fairly short fuse and was known to 'blow his top' under moderate provocation. Photography was Jack's passion and although I knew a little about this wonderful addition to any school's curriculum I became proficient under Jack's tutelage. Through Jack, this later became one of my contributions to schools, and I went on to help found various national examinations. It was always, in my humble opinion, one of the most attractive of subjects for both boys and girls, as many local photographers will agree.

George White was the second Deputy Head. I did not get to know him well but he impressed me as a quiet, reserved Scot. He was tall and handsome and had a fine voice with a soft accent. I mention him only in passing to dwell briefly on his strange departure from these shores. Arthur and George used to meet at school towards the end of those long summer holidays to 'knock out' a timetable for us all. How simple they were in those far-off fifties. On the final occasion Arthur awaited the customary phone call from George, neither of them having cars. None was forthcoming so Arthur tried George's home number at La Moye school house where he lived. Failing to get a response after several attempts, Arthur took a cab to La Moye and getting no reply to the doorbell, he took it upon himself to peep in at a window. The house was devoid of all furnishings. George had gone. No notice had been given or any intimation to any member of the staff. It was later thought that he had taken a post in his homeland and was never heard of again otherwise.

The staff meeting? Ah yes, I must learn to keep to my script and not wander off! We all soon learned that this was the beginning of a revolution in the island education system. The Elementary School and its traditions were dead. In its place specialist staff were responsible for subjects and boys packed their books away at the end of each lesson and changed rooms, to learn geography or whatever, instead of going on steadily with the same teacher from nine till four. There was a feeling of participation in an exciting development. We were well led by John Le Marquand, the President of the Public Instruction Committee and his Chief Officer, Charles Wimberley. Others have written at length about these fine educationalists, the practical businessman balanced by the sincere intellectual. Arthur Downer was a key mover and was always about his school encouraging and if need be, correcting. I enjoyed his visits to my

We too Remember When...

lessons. He always wore a dark three-piece suit and liked to speak to the boys with his jacket unbuttoned and his thumbs tucked into the armholes of his waistcoat. It was his favourite stance.

I know Jurat Downer, as he later became, will forgive me if I just mention *en passant* a little incident which gave all the staff at New Street – for we still referred to the two buildings by their original names - although now one school – some amusement. The staff room was a lively room with much going on. Arthur had decided that all the staff must keep Forecast Books to outline our lessons with aims and objectives clearly stated. These hard cover ring files were to be on the Deputy Head's desk last thing on Friday afternoon without fail, and when returned on Monday morning we found that a neat rubber stamp, about an inch square, had been employed to stamp each page with 'Examined by Headmaster'. This was a nuisance before the days of the current streams of paper landing on each teacher's desk. One day after many weeks of forecasting, some unknown wag on the staff managed to obtain the dreaded stamp and on a Monday morning many most unlikely surfaces had been adorned with 'Examined by Headmaster'. I cannot now recall many examples of such headmasterly diligence but I can clearly see today, forty years after the event, the mark of approval in each and every toilet bowl. The Forecast Books lingered a little longer, then fell into disuse.

My best friend to this day is Michael Hubbard, who was my opposite number in the school and Head of Art. We met on the way into La Motte Street School just as I was parking my car in James Street long before the days of yellow lines and traffic management schemes. We were not on the same staff, so to speak, for while he serviced La Motte Street I entertained my classes at New Street. Arthur decided to stir things up a bit and moved us to the opposite schools and so I found myself at La Motte Street in the upstairs Art Room with a view down onto the busy street below. Michael meanwhile took over my nautical Art Room at New Street which I always said had been floored by an out-of-work shipwright, for the floor curved gently upwards from two sides to the highest point at the middle like the deck of a ship. The interesting effect this had was to cause all the desks to lean outwards in sympathy.

I remember many of the boys and still meet them around Jersey. It has always amused me how, when I go into a business in search of some necessity, I come across some grown man speaking in normal tones with his colleagues but who immediately alters his demeanour on noticing me and speaks in almost halting, insecure, boyish accents "Hello Mr

Harris. How are you?" Many of the boys became very successful in a wide variety of careers even to the dizzy heights of members of the States of Jersey.

However, they could take you down a peg or two. I prepared my English lesson on Henry V most carefully and even borrowed, from Michael, his 78 r.p.m. records of Walton's wonderful music which accompanied the recent film starring Laurence Olivier. At the end of a spellbinding (in my opinion) hour of this masterpiece, I fell back into my chair and asked for questions. After some hesitation one hand went up. It was Bryan Druce, one of the best sportsmen in the school.

"Yes Bryan?"

He stood up, as was *de riguer* in those far-off days of polite behaviour. "Sir," he said, "I like it and all that but what's it got to do with English?" Discomfiture of over-enthusiastic teacher!

There were many events to interrupt the school day. Empire Day was still kept. Half-days were the largesse of the Head who would sometimes give a half-day holiday so that the boys could go swimming in really fine weather and many other *cause célèbre*. It was the unexpectedness of it that was most refreshing. How many parents today would rush to the phone to vent their feelings if their offspring should come home unexpectedly at the whim of the Headmaster? How many letters would be written to the Editor? Yet in those days this was quietly accepted.

Another diversion which staff, and boys, enjoyed was any exhibition of schoolwork. There was more time spent on preparing for this public exhibition of our work than on schoolwork itself. At the time of the Festival of Britain, I think it was, we created our own 'Skylon' in the school hall at La Motte Street, also the crown jewels and many other stately artefacts, in card and glue liberally daubed with paint. The school barely functioned as the doors were opened and the public, and many other accompanied 'crocodiles' of children from neighbouring schools, trooped in to be suitably awed by our handicraft.

And so it seemed it would go on forever until that day came when we were told about the plans for the new school to be built at d'Hautrée, the lovely house on St. Saviour's Hill. I recall the many journeys backwards and forwards carrying schoolbooks in my little Sunbeam Ten. It was at about this time too, that I dropped a very heavy plaster slab onto my big toe and had to be taken to the Casualty Department at the General Hospital where a broken bone was set. I did not see much of school for a week or so.

We too Remember When...

In 1956 we all moved lock, stock and barrel to d'Hautrée, to a new school of the best design. School uniform was introduced and specialist rooms became truly amazing with the latest equipment beautifully installed. A new era had begun but, do you know, many of us, boys and staff alike, still remember the old schools, La Motte Street and New Street, with fond reflections of 'another time'.

Do you remember the States Technical College of Housecraft in Phillips Street – where the Art Centre now stands?

The building didn't look very big from the outside but it was very deceptive. You walked into a little courtyard and then on the right was the caretakers', Mr and Mrs Dawkins, cottage. Facing the entrance, and surrounding the courtyard, was the main building where there were many rooms which were lettered, for example, 'Kitchen A', 'Kitchen B' and so on. Mine was 'Kitchen D', a lovely room, which was very large. They were all large, fairly modern rooms with lots of tables, several modern cookers – gas and electricity – and equipment like mixers and blenders.

On the left of the courtyard were the offices for the Principal and her secretary, and 'Kitchen A'. That was where Hotel and Catering was born, in 'Kitchen A'. That was how it all started for of course there was no Highlands then. Miss Hughes was involved in that side of the college, with the collaboration of Mr Schindler, who is now head of Curriculum at Highlands. It wasn't a terribly popular career for a young person to want to go into but he was there to teach and encourage those of varying ages who wanted to take up the trade.

Upstairs there was a needlework room, for the girls were expected to learn all aspects of, what was then called, 'domestic science'. Miss Longdon was such a talented and creative mistress of needlework! I remember the staff room was also on that floor. The only thing I disliked about the building was the system of heating. The heaters were hung from the ceiling and if you were working underneath it could be very uncomfortable.

As a pupil, the first term was dedicated to making your apron and your little cap, well it was only a band really. Not everyone liked sewing but it was part of the curriculum so they had to do it. They were lovely aprons, very fresh looking checks, different coloured checks for each school. Rouge Bouillon had white and mauve I remember.

One thing that always comes to mind when thinking of those days was the so-called 'pig-bin'. Do you remember that? In the 'pig bin' you put all the peelings with the exception of rhubarb (you had to be very careful not to put rhubarb because it upset the pigs), then the farmers used to come and collect it. The bin had to be cleaned out afterwards of course – the girls were taught to clean everything.

The lessons were mainly cookery but they did learn quite a lot of hygiene and nutrition. That was the whole purpose of the College so that the pupils would understand what needed to be done in the home and kitchen, what to eat and how to plan meals.

My first encounter with the College was when I did some adult classes there. I gave some demonstrations of what they called 'Continental Cookery' but what was, really, mostly Italian. I went there through having taught Italian at evening classes which, in those days, were held at St. Helier Girls' School. Then in 1955, one of the teachers, I think her name was Mrs Bouchard, had gone to Africa for a term to join her husband, who was working there, so there was this vacancy. I applied because I thought it would be a very good opportunity for me to further my teaching career.

I found it a fantastic experience. From the point of view of a teacher I found for and against the post. For, because I met so many girls from so many schools. It was quite an eye opener. There were girls from States and private schools, country and town, with the exception of the Girls' College who had set up their own. Against, well, being in an isolated building, detached from all of them, I could not share completely the life of any of the schools.

I taught girls from all the country schools – Rouge Bouillon, St. Helier Girls', the two Convents, the Collegiate, the Jersey High School and Helvetia – so as you can imagine I met a wide range of pupils from different backgrounds. In those days, if the pupils at the age of eleven were not chosen, shall we say, to go to one of the 'selective' schools, as Rouge Bouillon and Hautlieu were called then, they used to stay at their 'all ages' schools until they left at fifteen. They came to the college, with their ingredients, once a week for a morning or afternoon. We had demonstrations before the practical work or, if it was something simple, they would carry out the work under supervision.

One thing I must say is that the majority had those beautiful Jersey names. You don't seem to hear so many Jersey names now but there were so many then. In those days too, probably because of my foreign ear, I could distinguish accents. I could tell the difference between pupils from Grouville and St John's, for instance, and quite a lot of them communicated in Jersey French.

The Principal, Mrs Charlotte Bingham, was very firm. She reminded me very much of the Queen Mother, you know, that kind of deportment and sweet smile. Then there was Miss Hughes, Miss Evans, Miss Longdon, amongst the series of different teachers who came to teach there. Jennifer Gaudin was the secretary. It was a wonderful term and for me that was considered to end when the teacher came back.

I continued with my Italian classes, which I thoroughly enjoyed. At one time Mr Crill, who later became the island's Bailiff and was knighted, was one of the students. He sings very beautifully and I think he might have wanted to pronounce the Italian arias correctly. He only came to me for a short time because of course he was a very busy man. Another local singer who came to me was Mr Osborne Smith. He also had a beautiful voice.

Then after two terms break Mrs Bouchard (I hope I've remembered her name correctly, as I heard it pronounced, but I might well have misunderstood), anyway the teacher decided to return to Africa and the post became vacant, so I applied and was fortunate enough to get it. It was full-time teaching. In a normal secondary school you get your 'free' periods but there, with the different schools attending the classes each day you were teaching all the time.

I always insisted that we had good, up to date, equipment even though it might be new to some of the girls, they could experiment and learn how to use what was on the market and strive to attain that in the future. We were very lucky because the Electricity and Gas Companies always supplied us with excellent equipment free of charge but then when you think about it, it was a very good idea because you opened shop windows to the future adult, the future consumer. One person to whom I am indebted is Mr Brian Le Marquand, he was always so helpful. He used to come and demonstrate how to make bread or decorate a cake. We used to visit places like bakeries, the Dairy (now the Milk Marketing Board), Springside and so on. Gradually schools modernized. Beaulieu was, I think, one of the first to have their own 'Home Economics' classroom but they would come down to Phillips Street to sit their exams. Miss Hughes was the Principal by that time and she organized all that.

Cookery was a very popular subject with the girls but I thought, well, why not give boys a chance so I suggested we offer it to them. In collaboration with the Principal (by this time it was Mrs Hughes) and Mr Challinor, the Headmaster of St. Peter's School, the plans went ahead. I thought we would call it a 'Survivors Course', where I would teach them not only how to cook good food and know about nutrition but also know how to wash dishes and press their trousers, wash and iron their shirts, and so on. So the first boys came from St. Peter's School. About fourteen years old they were, only a handful of them, because remember this was quite new but they were all keen to come.

There were twins, really macho boys, who used to bring such beautiful fresh farm ingredients from their home each week. One day they came wearing the most gorgeous pullovers, one in red and the other in blue.

They said, "Do you like our pullovers Mrs Webb?"

"They're wonderful," I replied. "Your mother's been busy knitting."

"Oh, we knitted them!" they chorused.

Under their mother's guidance they had knitted their own pullovers!

There was another boy, physically not very big but very talented, who came to me one day and asked,

"Mrs Webb, do you think I could make a cake for my sister's first birthday?"

"Of course you can," I told him. "We'll make a sponge and ice it."

I can't say icing is my favourite thing but I didn't want to stop any child from making anything they wanted, provided they had the time. So he made it and iced it and I asked him,

"What would you like to write on it, shall we just put 'Jean' and add a candle?"

"Oh! No!" he said. "I want to put 'Happy Birthday Jean'."

"Do you think you'll have time?" I asked worriedly.

"Oh! Yes!" he replied confidently. And do you know he made a beautiful job of it. I don't think I could have done it better.

Then there was another one who was also very talented so I spoke to the Manager of the L'Horizon and asked if they'd like to give the boy a chance to practice during the holidays. They were not allowed to pay him, you see children could go into establishments but they could not be paid. Well they were so impressed with this boy that when he left they gave him a full set of chef's knives. We could see him flourish at Westminster College and encouraged him, but he had to work extremely hard to reach this goal. However he got there and he did well, went on to

We too Remember When...

Switzerland, and is back in the island now. At Phillips Street the boys had enjoyed being 'different'. They washed the dishes, ironed and cleaned as well as learning to cook. And why shouldn't they be given a chance? I enjoyed teaching boys home-crafts, they are very practical and you can laugh with them.

I remember one of the boys, having washed and ironed his shirt, showed it to me and asked me if he could wear it that night.

"Of course you can wear it tonight, you can wear it now if you like, but why tonight?"

The other boys sniggered, "Because he's going out with his bird!"

Happy memories!

Mrs Stefania Webb

Remember St. James' School?

I got the appointment to St. James in '68. There was a vacancy because Nick Herbert, Jim Kezourec and two other members of staff were going to Plat Douet to open the new school so that left St. James bereft of staff. I do know, when we got there, that the parents were rather anxious, having lost so many staff.

Eric McWhinney was the Head and he appointed me as his Deputy Head Teacher. He was very shrewd in his other appointments. Three lovely ladies came. Miss James, a Welsh girl, Miss Rose, an English girl and Miss Birse who was Scottish. Nick Herbert had left a lovely carry-on, the children were... ooh!.... delightful. There was a routine that they knew. What an atmosphere he left. Industry was the key word. The drawback was the building itself and yet, it sounds paradoxical, but this drawback was advantageous for it created a family atmosphere. You had four classrooms and you'd to go through each one if you wanted to go out to the toilets. And if you wanted to visit anyone, from the entrance, you'd to go through everybody's room so you interrupted everything. As years went by though the children just ignored people going through, they were that busy and occupied. That was an advantage but in fact some people wondered if we were being rude at times, not answering them as they went through, because we were so used to people going by.

I was Deputy Head and as a teacher I had my own class. We were appointed in January 1968 so one term had already gone of the school year, that's why the parents were very anxious. There was a thriving

St. James' School, 1983.

P.T.A. but it wasn't very long before they realised that things were carrying on as before and while, as the years went on, some things were added, some were taken away.

Eric McWhinney was promoted to Grouville in 1971. He left us a term or two without a Head so I became Acting Head. Later that year they appointed me Headteacher. We needed a Deputy Head of course and that was the best thing that happened to me because they appointed Faith Herbert, Nick's wife. She was absolutely outstanding.

At separate times Faith and Mrs Pat Small were responsible for a small class of children who had specific needs. This was a great success due to these two dedicated teachers because we eventually returned these children back into the mainstream classes. We had a good cross-section of children from the area because we were part-townie. We had our share of families in need. We did a little survey at one time and we found that approximately a third of the families within the school had some form of problem at home whether it was one parent or whatever. Many of them found stability within school because of the lack of it elsewhere. It was a particularly happy school. Very. You ask the parents.

We had about, I'm guessing again, but we had about 120 children when we started and for reasons I've forgotten about, maybe there was movement into the area, changes in catchment areas, it got up to 163 at one time. And we'd only four normal sized rooms plus two small ones! We spread ourselves to the caretaker's cottage. The caretaker's cottage was at the back but it was a bit of a horror because you had to climb a spiral staircase to get to our additional classroom. I took the more senior class up there and they were very responsible. Again they had separate rooms so the guy in charge, Mr Sheehan, he put those that were of, you

We too Remember When...

know, reputable character, in the room where they didn't need his constant attention whilst he stayed with the others.

The most important part of the school for me was the Infant Department. It was such a good, solid foundation and the staff were prepared to work. They were grand. People moved on of course but the Infant Department was the basis. And then there was the setting up of a really good extended reading scheme by Faith and others on the staff and that took us still further. By the time the children reached the top class they were given set tasks and they got on with them without any fuss. If you ask Senior schools, even today, they can identify where Primary children come from by their attitude to work.

We had no hall, no on site facilities for P.E. or anything, but one year we won the Smaller Schools' Athletics Cup. In 1976, I can't remember exactly now but it was something to do with the Bicentennial of the U.S.A., the Primary schools were invited to take part in a competition. Again I'm vague about the details but Deputy Smale and his travel company were part of it because they took the eventual winners to London. You'd to set up your own ideas about the bicentennial. We did it as it was with the Pilgrim Fathers, how it is today, and how it might be in the future. It was all done after school, more than in school time, so it was an additional task. There were three teachers that really worked hard on that. Mrs Herbert, Miss Wilson and Therese Murray, she's now Mrs Renouf. (She's a peripatetic, she goes round to schools today.) Eventually we won the competition. The smallest school in the island! The group involved won a trip to London.

We took the children away on school trips. That was another feature of school life. I got the idea after chatting with Derek Le Maistre and Roland Heaven. Derek's school, First Tower, used to go to France. Well we tried it twice but it wasn't right for our children, too expensive. The Education Committee was keen for schools to go to France but the pockets of our parents couldn't meet it. I devised a savings scheme so that when the children started school in the infants the parents were told about this and they could save right through the years. By the time their child got to years four, five and six the money would be there. We were hopeful that everyone would be able to go and for those who still struggled I went to see certain individuals in the Variety Club. They helped out generously.

We enjoyed taking them to England best. We asked Education for the loan of the mini buses and we had some lovely trips. The best area was around Bournemouth. Everything we could find, like railway lines, rivers, things our children never got an opportunity to see in Jersey, we took them to. Plymouth...Dartmoor was a good visit...and the cathedrals of Wells and Exeter. All to do with history. In fact one year, we had a good time but it was all too much. We went to England and travelled from youth hostel to youth hostel in about four or five days but there were too many moves at once. However the children were great. They stacked the bus. It was rather like the old stage coach days when they piled the luggage on top and went from place to place!

We wouldn't allow any nonsense, in fact, on early trips when you were still able to discipline them in a certain way, one or two of them were punished for their misbehaviour.

They soon complied. We always had two bus loads, Keith Sheehan and I were the drivers, and we took one other female member of staff to accompany us. He was a rock, Keith Sheehan. In fact it was the two of us, and Roland Heaven, that initiated ideas to set up the rules and regulations for future school visits. You had to make sure that you did things right and safely.

We were always complimented on the behaviour of Jersey children. When they went abroad their behaviour was exemplary. We were always being complimented. Every evening we used to gather around the piano at the hotel and have a singsong because the top class was principally the choir of the school. The proprietors and the people staying at the hotel used to have an impromptu, and free, concert each evening.

Another feature was at Christmas. Every class did a presentation and because it was a collection of presentations we called it, 'Christmas Cracker.' We took the partition back and used two rooms. One year we dressed up and had to walk around the outside of the building to come in on the stage that we built up on blocks from the Education department! I was on the piano in a little cubby hole at the top of some stairs so that the stage was free. Well, that was because the first time we'd put the piano on the stage we'd found that it took up too much room, so they closeted me in there! It rained one night so we had to rearrange things so that we came in through the classrooms, past parents! It all added to the fun! The highlight was the Staff's contribution to 'The Christmas Cracker.'

We didn't have visits from the school inspectors too often but when they came they spoke highly of our work programmes and always commented on the friendly discipline and how our children set about

We too Remember When...

Iain Nutter with the Summer B League Joint Champions, 1985.

their tasks diligently and willingly. Oh! It was a very happy time.

Then the years passed and in 1983 the school was to be closed and joined together with St. Luke's. The two schools were to be merged.

Iain Nutter

Kay Wills née Blampied recalls...

I was born in South Africa, but all my relations are Jersey. My mother wasn't born in Jersey either but her parents were. My father was but he went out to South Africa as a young man and met my mother. That was funny wasn't it? Jersey stock meeting up on the other side of the world! There's a big Jersey connection in South Africa. A lot of my family went out there because my grandparents were seafaring captains, you see.

I didn't grow up in South Africa. My father came back to take over his father's business, George Blampied, Merchants, which was on the Esplanade. To start with we lived in Dicq Road. Though I am an only child I wasn't spoilt. My parents were very strict. When it came to coming home my father insisted I had to be home every night by nine o'clock. That was even when I was engaged!

How did we meet our boyfriends? Well, I suppose it was chiefly through tennis and sport. You used to have your boyfriends meeting you when you went down to the F.B. Fields for a game of hockey. The Boys' Modern School, which stood on the old Ritz Hotel site in Colomberie, was very popular with girls from the Collegiate, and at the end of a day at the F.B. any boyfriends would be waiting to walk us home. I had wonderful parents who thought that 'it was no good having any under counter business' so I used to be able to bring them home. I had parties. They were very modern that way. Though I was an only child I wasn't a lonely one because I was encouraged to be sociable.

By this time my parents had bought the family property in Trinity, in the area where my father was born. I liked living there though of course soon afterwards I went across to England. You see I'd trained with Marjorie Pye, here in Jersey, went away to finish my education with drama at the Guildhall School of Music and I qualified from there. Then came plenty of opportunities. At that time I could have got many jobs, acting and that, in England but I didn't want to. Production was my side you see.

When I came back from studying at the Guildhall School of Music my father bought me a car, a Singer. I'll always remember that! Then I had a Standard. I can remember driving it to a game of badminton one evening and not having a clue how to turn the lights on! I didn't have a Driving Test. You learnt to drive and whoever was teaching you vouched that you could! I can also remember coming face to face with a horse and cart and being afraid to reverse and telling the driver to 'go back because it's easier to push a horse back that a car!'

I had to take a test when I went to London later though, a very severe A.A.Test. All through London! My father was so proud when I passed.

❧

I learnt to drive at seventeen. I didn't have a test either. A week after my birthday I went up to Sydney Crill's office in Hill Street (he was the Constable of St. Clement) and said I wanted a driving licence. His clerk asked my age and address before writing out the licence and then, just before handing it to me he said, "Oh, you can drive by the way?"

I replied, "Yes, I've had lessons."

"Well that's all right then!" he said. And of course there were no traffic lights then, no yellow lines. You had to be careful coming out of a by-road because there were no signs to tell you what it was. I think people

We too Remember When...

drove more carefully then, and of course there wasn't the speed. There weren't the accidents we hear of today.

I remember when my Dad bought his very first car in 1932. The registration number was 7312. I'll always remember that. So his was only the 7,312th registration! But of course there weren't that number of cars on the island.

My first car was a second-hand little Morris Eight. I paid £65, but when it had to be handed in during the Occupation my Dad was given a cheque for £70! When we returned I found I'd made £5 on the deal! Mind you that car, in those days, would only have cost about £125 - £130 new.

In 1948 I bought a brand new Morris Minor, from Colbacks in the Parade, for £190. It was a lovely little car, a four-door saloon.

Pat Letto

I was riding this motor bike with my pillion rider and what do I see coming towards us but a hay cart. It filled the whole lane. I nearly closed my eyes as I drove through the narrow gap and when we came out the other side we looked like haystacks ourselves! I had the presence of mind to go up the escape road and as I got off I said to Ted, my pillion rider,

"You can do the hair-pin bend. I'm not driving any more today!"

I don't think I had the pluck to drive again for a while. That bike was an old Douglas two and three-quarter, quick start. Then a friend, Lil Le Quesne, told Mr Laurens that I rode a motor bike and he thought I'd be quite cheap to have as a driver for the firm so he paid for my licence. That was all of ten shillings and it was for life. Not renewable – for life! The test? Well, the first thing I learnt was that the van I was going to drive had no indicators, no mirrors, and the back was solid. So if you wanted to see what was behind you had to put your head out of the window! It was a hideous thing, either green with red lettering on it or the other way around. Anyway the fella that taught me to drive said,

"Ah! let's not take that darn van. I've got a two-seater, you could use that and take your test in it."

Well, it was a bit different to say the least. A Ford it was. The gears were the same and he was allowed to sit in the little dicky seat at the back. The examiner, I don't think he'd even ridden a bicycle never mind a car, sat beside me. I had to go up the left hand side of the Parade, round Elizabeth Place, and down where Cyril Le Marquand House is now.

Daff Noël

There were no indicators so I had to put out my hand and watch for the traffic when I was crossing. I can see me now. I drew up outside the Town Hall quite well and had my licence given me right away. Unfortunately I didn't drive long enough to know what my full potential might have been for I only drove for seven months. I got married you see.

Rosa Borny

John Day *remembers...*

This is a photograph of me in my cycle car Carden, taken outside our shop, Day's, in Bath Street. The Carden has wooden mudguards and gas lighting. There are only two of these cars in the world, the other is in America. It's being garaged by the Motor Museum. You couldn't go on the road with it now, it hasn't any wheel brakes.

(Reproduced by kind permission of *The Jersey Evening Post*)

With the business, we didn't have much time for going out but I bought a van and converted it. The children and my father-in-law used to love outings to the sand dunes at St. Ouen's. We had some excitement down there though. One afternoon, it must have been about six o'clock, something like that, my wife and the girls had had their tea and went off to get an ice-cream, some distance away. Thankfully my father-in-law had got out of the van for, I don't know whether I saw them coming back but, I started to move. The sand gave way and over the van went, on my side. It gathered momentum and went over three or four times and when it came to a stop I was covered in what I thought was blood. It was battery acid from a battery that had been thrown around inside the van. My shirt was all burnt. I ran down into the tide and washed myself off!! The other thing that had been flying about inside the van was one of those little Electrolux fridges. You should have seen the bulges in the sides of the van where it had bounced! Our eldest girl was quite upset by it all.

Do you remember when the firemen and their families lived and worked, from the old Fire Station in Nelson Street? **Pat Williams, née Le Masurier** *looks back...*

My father served as Secretary to five Constables of St. Helier, retiring (at sixty-two) in 1940 at the start of the Occupation. When the Germans raised the Swastika over the Town Hall he felt he could not continue to work there.

I particularly remember Constable Cumming, who was in office at the beginning of the Occupation, as he lived next door to us in Beach Road, also the ex-Constable John Pinel, who later became the Police Court Magistrate. My father and I used to go and visit him and his wife and niece. By that time we had moved to live on Victoria Avenue and become a neighbour of his. He seemed lively and charming to me and was, I have heard, quite a character.

Whether it was because of my father's job or not I don't know, but he was also Secretary of the Fire Brigade for many years so I used to spend a lot of time at the Old Fire Station. My father could go back to the time before they built the Station in Nelson Street, when they had the horse-drawn engines based at the Town Hall. He'd built up a close friendship with Joe Remphry and his family, who I always knew as Chief Officer of the Fire Brigade.

I remember the caretakers, the Carters, had a flat over what was called the watch-room. They had four children and, when they went away for the Occupation, the Pinels (Mr Pinel was a fireman) moved into the flat to act as caretakers.

There was a cottage where Mr Remphry, the Chief Officer (I used to call him Joe-Joe) lived with his wife (Granny) and their daughter Dorothy, (a much loved 'Aunty Dolly' to many). She was married to Louis Ledo, who became a fireman at the start of the Occupation and continued as one until his retirement. Their single depth cottage was right down in the corner of the yard, facing up at the Station. It backed on to the houses at the top of Halkett Place. They had a sort of a scullery/kitchen with a bath in it and a living room, I suppose it would have been, with an open fire in a black range.

Across the passage, on the other side of the front door, was a room they used for best. They put a fire in there at Christmas and when Louis Ledo's parents and an aunt visited they always sat in that best room. Directly above this room was the bedroom where Uncle Louis and Aunty Dolly, as I used to call them, slept. Then there was the Remphrys', Joe-Joe and Granny's, bedroom. On top of the scullery there was another bedroom. Above again, right at the top of the stairs was one attic. No bathroom and, for the loo, you had to go right outside, and around the house. It was beside the coal hole. There was a hen house, with a run down along the side as well. Granny Remphry used to keep chickens and breed turkeys for Christmas. As you can see from the photograph they used to run free at times. Denis Carter, who is with me in the photo, returned to Jersey after the war with his wife Mabs. He became a fireman also, rising through the ranks of the Brigade. Sadly he is now dead.

We lived in Beach Road and they tell me that, before the war when I was quite young, I used to walk from Beach Road to Colomberie, where Le Riches used to be, and the traffic control man would see me across the road. I would then carry on to the Fire Station. Do you remember how the wall at the entrance to the yard used to be covered in loganberries? Granny Remphry used to pick them and sell them.

My father had a car quite early on but we had no garage in Beach Road so he used to keep it at the station. Then one of them – either Joe-Joe, or Uncle Louis – would drive the car down to our house on a Thursday afternoon and my father would drive me, my mother and aunt, out. The

We too Remember When...

same on Sundays. Then the car would go back to the station. It was there all through the Occupation.

I remember, while I was at the J.C.G. (Jersey College For Girls), I used to go to the station every day after school. There was always so much life there. Everybody who lived in and around town knew the Remphrys and Louis and Dolly Ledo. They were very friendly people and would do anything for anyone. They adored children. It was a pity they never had any of their own. There was always so much going on around them and people always called cheery 'hellos' or stopped to chat as they were walking through the yard.

Aunty Dolly was a dressmaker and she used to make some of my clothes. She even made my son a towelling robe for school. My mother used to knit. I remember Aunty Dolly had a jumper that my mother knitted her. It was pale blue, with mauve and white stripes!

I remember too that I used to leave my bicycle in the lean-to shed they had and walk down to Wakehams in Bath Street to buy a sixpenny

Above: Dolly and Louis Ledo and Mr and Mrs Remphry.

Right: Pat having fun with the chickens that roamed free in the station yard.

Daff Noël

Denis Carter and Pat posing with one of the chickens.

Eldorado. I had to come back and eat it because in those days we weren't allowed to eat in the street. The College was very strict. You got an 'Order Mark' for not wearing your beret in the street! I can't say I loved the College. I didn't mind it but I was very average and wasn't very sporty. I loathed going up to the top of La Pouquelaye to play hockey. It was freezing cold!

There was another fireman that I remember, Jack Vautier, who used to drive the ambulance. They kept the ambulance at the station too. The men used to interchange between driving the ambulance and fire engine.

I think it was probably after the second Le Gallais fire that 'they' realised how old Chief Officer Joe Remphry, who had carried the Brigade all through the difficult years of the Occupation, was. I'm not sure of his age but he must have been well past retirement, (as we know it now!) so he retired, and a new Chief Officer, Frank Edmonston, came from Manchester in 1950. It must have been good for Joe-Joe – he didn't have to move away from the Station and could continue to be in the 'centre of things', talking to the firemen and people walking through the yard, especially after Granny Remphry had died.

❧

When we had a fire at our house, Rosedale, in St. Clements, I said to the Fire Chief, Mr Edmonston, "Come in love and have a cup of tea."

He said, "Nay lass, I'll put your fire out first!"

Peggy Swain

❧

We too Remember When...

I was born at Anstruther Villa, Dicq Road, St. Saviour in January 1920. I had two sisters, Violet who was born in 1914 and Kathleen who was born in 1910. Violet died in 1934 and Kathleen in 1987. We were a very happy family. My mother died in 1957 and my father fourteen weeks after in 1958.

When I was two years old we went to live out at 'Sea Breeze', La Moye. It had sea views to Noirmont Point, Corbière and, on a clear day, Guernsey and Sark. The old signal station stood on our property. There was also a very tall flag post and, when we visited there weekly, father used to dip the flag when mail boats were passing and they would sound their sirens in reply.

We sold the property about twelve years ago. It was unoccupied for a while after being let and, as it was empty, was being vandalised. It was becoming a worry to my sister and myself. I loved La Moye, it was then so free of buildings, the wild flowers and gorse growing in abundance.

We returned to St. Saviour when I was six or seven years old. We lived in Plaisance Terrace, on what is now known as La Route Du Fort. Violet died whilst we were living there so shortly afterwards we moved as there were too many sad memories. We then moved to Green Road where I am still living.

I was educated at Colomberie House School. I spent my eleven years there. It was a lovely school, everyone was so nice and friendly. I still belong to the Old Girls' Association. Hockey and tennis were my favourite sports. I continued to play tennis for many years after leaving school.

Three days after leaving school in 1937 I started work at McKee's Music Shop in Beresford Street. From a very small girl I had longed to work in a music shop. My dream came true. Unfortunately a short time after starting work war broke out and I was suspended until Mr McKee decided what to do about the business. He then asked me to return to make up the accounts for piano tuning and sale of second-hand music, etc. As there was little future there I obtained work in an insurance company, where I stayed for several years.

I became a member of the Jersey Green Room Club in 1942, playing the piano in the orchestra and being in the singing chorus for 'The King And I', 'South Pacific', 'Merry Widow' and many other musicals. The orchestras were under the direction of Mr Lyndon Marguerie, later Dr. Marguerie, Mr Norman Blake and Mr J.B. McNair.

My pianoforte teacher was Mr Walter Williams, who trained me up to my Associated Board Advanced Grade, also my singing exams. Then Mr

Leonard Herivel prepared me for my final grades in both piano and singing. He also prepared me for my Trinity College Performers exam which I unfortunately failed by two marks. Having had the required marks for my Associated Board final singing exam Mr Herivel applied for me to try for a scholarship, but owing to the Occupation of Jersey I was two years too old to be considered.

I am a retired Civil Servant having worked for the Judicial Greffe and States Greffe for nearly twenty years.

My hobbies include gardening and I am a member of the Jersey Island Singers. I love playing the piano and church organs and was Organist at St. Luke's Church for eleven years. I am also a member of the St. Luke's Ladies Guild and St. Clement's Women's Institute and attend whist drives once or twice weekly.

Myra Hunt

Robert Le Brocq, Constable of St. Helier, was born in 1937...

I believe my twin Lester and I were conceived in St. Ouen's, though we were born in Millbrook Nursing Home! We are the youngest of nine children. Eight boys and one girl, Yvonne. She was in the middle. My father didn't believe she was a girl until he removed the nappy! She was the apple of his eye.

We lived at Spring Valley Farm, St. Ouen's which is at La Creux Baillot. It was a big, granite farmhouse, part rendered in the front. There were two principal rooms, a dining room and a lounge, or front room as we used to call it, a wing on the side at the back with a wash house, a bathroom downstairs and the kitchen. There was a big oil painting on the stairs that my mother bought and then upstairs there were four bedrooms and, upstairs again, attic bedrooms. With nine children the house had to be fairly big.

Outside you went down one side of the farm buildings and, in the middle, was the horse stable, cow barn and the feed store. Then you went down the bottom of the yard and you came upon the pigsties. As you came up again there was the potato store, the machinery store, the store where they kept all the cider, the dairy and the staff cottages.

Most of my brothers are very involved in farming and I would say I certainly enjoyed the farm. It's situated at the top of the valley that

We too Remember When...

The Le Brocq children.

runs all the way down to Grève De Lecq woods where we used to play. Life was great.

My father had a large Studebaker in which he used to take all the family out on Sundays. We'd all be dressed in white. White shirts, white trousers and red tie. Unfortunately my parents separated and my mother left the farm during the war. We stayed on for a short time and when she got a house in town the five youngest of us went to live with her. I would have been about two or three at the time but my mother never prevented us from going back to the farm to see our father and elder brothers, in fact she encouraged us really. I have very good memories of the farm. I enjoyed the haymaking, playing in the straw and all that sort of thing.

Everything was done by hand in those days, with the horse and the shearers. They didn't have the machinery they have today. All the neighbours used to come in and help with the haymaking, staying for a meal afterwards. It was a good part of my childhood, the times I spent on the farm. There was fantastic freedom, no traffic, no cars to worry about. We had such a very large playground with all the fields around the farm and the woods.

There was a farm called Newlands which my uncle Jim lived in and a French lady, Madame Glot, my twin's Godmother, had a cottage off that. She'd been with the family all through from working with my grandparents. We often used to go out on Sunday morning and stay with her. We'd get out St. Ouen's about half-past ten, stay with her the rest of the day before going down on the farm, mucking about. Across the road from her cottage was Le Chataigniers where my cousin Jim, who was Constable of St. Ouen, lived and alongside of that, La Chasse, where my granny and Uncle Hedley lived. Our farm, Spring Valley, was around the corner. It meant we had all three families living on farms close by. When we visited we'd take the number 7 bus to St. Ouen's, get off at the junction alongside the Telecoms station, go and see Madame Glot, then Uncle Jim, and finally we'd call in on Granny Le Brocq, before going to see my Dad and helping around the farm.

Each of my brothers had a job around the farm. Dennis, the eldest, was very interested in the growing side, Graham was very keen on the horses, he did the showing and the show jumping. Unfortunately he has passed away. Vernon did the jobs around the farm and though Leslie was training to be a carpenter he still had to do his bit around the farm as well. They used to rotate who did the milking because in those days they milked by hand and even when they got milking machines they still had to rotate. They all had jobs to do, as I say, but not us younger ones – Brian, Yvonne, David, Lester and myself. In town Mum used to send us on messages, before and after school, and we'd do messages for old people, but that was all.

During the war we younger ones and Mum, lived at various addresses. The first one was near St. Simon's Church in Great Union Road and then we moved to New Street, three doors away from where Mr Day's business is now. Then we moved to St. Saviour's Road, at the bottom of Woodville Avenue, where I can remember playing on the step while they moved in all the furniture.

The very first time I went to school was at Brighton Road and that was to get an injection, so I really didn't like school after that! I think that's one of the biggest mistakes anyone can make, to take a child to a school and give them an injection, because it really puts them off. Unfortunately, after that first, short visit, my schooling was rather disrupted.

I started off in the infant department of Brighton Road and from there went to Halkett Place, then St. Ouen's. I do remember I moved on again to St. James, from St. James to La Motte Street, La Motte Street back to St. James and then, when they changed the name of La Motte Street to St. Helier Secondary Boys' I went back there! (I took the exam for Hautlieu and qualified but I didn't go, which I regret, but the changes in education came when I was fifteen and, with my mother not being well off, it was time for me to start work.)

We too Remember When...

Mrs Le Rue was the Head of St. James then. She was a strict disciplinarian. The school at that time was very much attached to the church, being right next door, so I was also in the Church choir ....No, I don't sing now. I was only in it for the 2/6d a month! I remember the Vicar of St. James, Reverend Robinson. Lovely vicar.

The twins, centre front, in the St. James' Church Choir.

Mr Dauthrea was the Headmaster of La Motte Street at first, then Mr Downer took over. He came from St. Ouen's so he knew us. We were known as the terrible twins! Our teacher was Miss Le Breton, she was a lovely teacher. Her brother was the Truant Officer. Lester and I looked extremely alike and were always protective of each other. I remember one day Lester was called out and given the cane. He asked what it was for. When Mrs Le Breton told him and he said,

"But it wasn't me Miss, it was my brother!"

Well, I escaped that day but I wasn't the star pupil. I think I got the cane off of every teacher in the school, either the cane, or the slipper. You would also be sent out to the Headmaster for two strokes of the cane, you'd wait in the hallway outside his office in trepidation. We got punished for all sorts of harmless mischief but nothing to what the kids get up to today. I don't think it did me any harm and I don't think I ever got the cane when I didn't deserve it, though not so my poor brother!

I believe in discipline. I feel one of the problems of society today is that we have too many nimby people who interfere. Teachers have an extremely difficult job to do and sometimes discipline is justified. I know that my mother had extreme difficulty in keeping discipline in the family,

Daff Noël

with eight boys and one girl. If they misbehaved...I can't remember it happening to me but... if they'd been naughty during the day, she would make them drop their pyjamas when they went to bed and go down the row of them with stinging nettles. She always said that it didn't leave a mark but it left a lot of pimples!

I had a break in all my education, when I went back out to St. Ouen's at one stage during the Occupation. There was an incident where my mother was detained by the Germans because she wouldn't give information regarding people who had stolen some sugar. We were taken to the hospital until our father could come into town to fetch us, which he did that night. I can clearly remember my twin brother and I sitting on a hospital bed, rolling up bandages. We went back to the farm, oh, for a couple of months I suppose.

The things that happened during the Occupation! I can remember one lunch hour, as we were making our way to St. Ouen's School, a bi-plane – an American reconnaissance plane I found out later – was weaving in and out above us. It was being fired at by the ack-ack and eventually the gunners got him. He actually baled out but I never found out what happened to him. Another thing that occurred at the farm...There was a young German, called Peter Schumaker, who used to bring his gun and ammunition and throw it all behind the door before going rabbiting with my brothers. He'd been conscripted into the Army, only about eighteen he was, and he wasn't at all interested in the war. He'd come from farming stock and got on very well with my brothers. There was a slit trench in a field across the road from the farm and that's where he was billeted.

When my mother came out of prison she took us back home. She used to run a lodging house, but things were still harder in town. One thing I remember was going down Havre des Pas with the old pram to get water, salt water, to be boiled up, and all in bare feet because you didn't wear your shoes in the summer, you kept them for the winter. I remember going up the cobbled Tunnel Street to the Gas Works to get the tar to make the fire burn and putting a bit of paper on the fire at the end of the evening so that we would have an extra bit of light to see by. We'd go up Victoria College for wood from the Italians, because the Woodville Hotel was billeted by both the Germans, and the Italians you know. We'd scrounge anything. My clothes were passed down from my older brothers of course, but you just made do. At the end of 1944 my overcoat was made out of a pale grey blanket!

We had a backyard where we used to keep chickens and rabbits. We

We too Remember When...

grew all sorts of vegetables. My twin and I used to grow tomatoes and, of course, we were responsible for feeding the chickens, bantams, and the rabbits. There was a bakehouse in Simon Place where we used to take our meal to be cooked, next door to Vardons (there's a photography shop there now).

During the war we lived in St. Saviour's Road and when there weren't any buses our neighbour, Mr Jennings, who had a charcoal lorry, would let us jump on the back and take us to St. Ouen's. It was part of his milk round. He had to go out in the morning so he used to drop us at the farm and pick us up on the way back. Imagine those two little urchins on the back of that lorry! We were quite safe but you wouldn't do that sort of thing now.

Just after the war my father became a reasonably big cattle and horse dealer so we had lots and lots of horses. I think he was the largest importer of horses in the island. My brothers used to take the horses down to Grève De Lecq of a Sunday morning for a wash and a trot on the beach. I didn't ride. I'd help get cattle ready for shows and keep the stables clean. There wasn't a straw out of place you know! No, I didn't show the cattle.

I can remember once, I suppose my twin brother and I would have been perhaps nine or ten, we were returning back through town after a trip to the farm and were looking at the big fruit display in a shop window in Halkett Street when a gentleman came up.

"If you had the money what would you choose," he asked.

"I'd like one of those big orange things," I said.

Well he bought me an orange but I didn't know how to peel it. I'd never had one. It was the same when I was given a banana. I didn't know how to peel that either!

We used to look in the shop windows and have little competitions trying to find the highest price. Everything in the shops was priced in those days and we learnt everything about goods and prices from those windows.

I was involved with the Scouts. My twin and I used to belong to the All Saints troop and I enjoyed that very much. The brothers who ran it were Reg, Bill and Ron Laurens. We went away camping to England once, I remember it because it was the first time I ever went away. It was at a time when one rarely left the island. We went to a farm on Southampton Water. I'm a great admirer of what the Scouts, and Guides, do for youngsters. They're very good organisations. They teach self-discipline

Daff Noël

The twins, Bob is on the right, in the Scouts.

and respect for others.

When I left school I was supposed to go and work for Mr Morel, the Seed Merchant in Cattle Street, where Norma Jeans night club is now. I had the job to work in the shop but just before I was due to start my mother said she thought I ought to learn a trade so I went to work for Horn Bros., the builders, in Winchester Street. Times were pretty hard then. I started my trade working a forty-five hour week. It worked out at fourpence halfpenny an hour! The boss, Mr Horn, was very good though. We used to finish at twelve o'clock on a Saturday and he'd say, "If you want to clean the garage out for me you can have an extra shilling."

It was a very large, double, garage-cum-store and I used to sweep it out for that extra shilling. Of the 27s. I earnt I used to give my mother £1 towards my keep and my clothes, and I had 7s. for myself. I moved about a bit because I went from Horn Bros. to work with my brother Leslie on roof tiling then moved again to C.W. Construction, who had been responsible for building Hautlieu School. I was with them for a while and, because I was buying a car, I also worked part-time for Bee-Line Taxis, remember them? Then I went to work for the Telephone Department as a cable joiner for five and a half years but the money at the Telephones wasn't very good and, as by this time I was married, I worked part-time for my brother David in the building line.

How did I meet my wife Eileen? My mother had gone into Overdale with a shadow of T.B. and I met her there, during the Queen's Speech, on Christmas Day 1958. She thought I had an affliction with my eye because I kept giving her the 'glad eye'! We got engaged the following June and married in the November.

The family are all reasonably close together, we're all in the island. We meet up once a year for dinner, something we promised Mum before she died. We always used to take her out on her birthday so we still meet up.

I never imagined I would be Constable for we were never taught about the Honorary System or local politics at school. I got involved in the Parish about eighteen years ago. At the time my wife and I were running a guest house in Royal Crescent (that was besides my building business – I've never been afraid of hard work!) and my twin brother Lester, who was a Constable's Officer, suggested I got involved in the Parish. So I came down, found out what it was about, and got elected as a Constable's Officer. After three years I applied for the vacancy of Centenier and was elected.

When Fred Clarke decided to retire as Constable I thought I might give it a go. I liked the idea of keeping the tradition in the family for we've had four Connétables in the family, three in St. Peter's and one in St. Ouen's. I'd like to think I would leave my mark. I don't find any difficulty in working fifty or sixty hours a week. I happen to enjoy what I do and when I stop enjoying it, I'll give it up.

Do you remember the General Hospital, before it was rebuilt and modernised? When the walls of the wards and corridors were all painted with two-colour gloss, green on the bottom and cream above. And the only necessary security was the man in the Porter's Lodge at the entrance in Gloucester Street? When the smell of disinfectant and ether, together with the forbidding faces of the senior medical staff, combined to intimidate. And the wards were large, the beds many, and 'waiting lists' were yet to be imported? When the Children's Ward had its own operating theatre, the hospital its own sewing workroom – where uniforms and bedding were both made and repaired. And meals were freshly cooked each day in the kitchens? When Matron's regime was unquestioned, the nurses not expected to do anything other than administer to the patients. And the Maternity Hospital was in St. Saviour's Road, the sanatorium and later convalescent home, was at Overdale? When everyone paid for medical and surgical treatment but private patients went into a nursing home. And a visit to the dentist?

Daff Noël

Arthur Stanley 'Stan' Swain, Dental Consultant at the General Hospital for 36 years, recalls...

Dental work, at the hospital, was completely free for the children. Adults could come and get a tooth out by gas and it would cost them three shillings. No fillings for grown-ups but surgical advice yes, and of course dentists would send patients down to the Hospital if it was something outside the normal dentists' scope.

My wife Peggy and I came to Jersey on holiday in 1946 and decided to stay. What decided us? Oh, I don't know. We could have gone anywhere, after all we're both from Sheffield. No, I think it was the beauty of the island and the pleasantness of the people. They seemed to take to us you know. It seems extraordinary that we happened to be in an Estate Agents, asking if they had any premises suitable for a dentist's surgery and being told 'No', when Phillip Benest was just coming through the front door. He was walking behind me, I didn't see him at first, and even then I just saw him out of the corner of my eye. He turned and came back and he said, "Did I hear you say 'dental surgery'?"

I said "Yes, I was looking for some rooms."

"Well," he said "It just so happens that the dentist across the road, next door to Boots, came in yesterday and said he was thinking of selling his dental practice. He's a man that's married a Jersey girl out in India, one of the Kempster family. She brought him back to Jersey to set up practice, when he'd got his discharge after the war, and now he's thinking of selling it. He's told me not to advertise it because he's negotiating for a practice in Columbo, in Ceylon, and he's not finalised that yet. But if he does buy that he'll be wanting to sell this one. Go across and see him. I know he's told me not to say but since you're here, well, it seems ridiculous not to go."

So I went across to see him and he nearly dropped through the floor. He says, "Well, you're here now and in two days I shall know whether I've purchased this other practice, so we'll make an appointment for then."

He had, and I got the practice. And he'd only been going twelve months, you know. The funny thing you see, was that a relation of his was one of the founder members of the Dental Manufacturing Company that made a lot of dental equipment, in fact it was the only one at one time. He had a pull at Headquarters to get all this equipment, at the time – just after the war – when it was very difficult. So I managed to get his drill, his chair, his lamp and an X-ray machine. It was all included. But there wasn't a big practice to sell because he'd not been here very long.

The permit I got to practice as a dentist is very simple, it even looks hand typed, but for all that it's a lifetime one. It gives me the remit to be a dentist, in Jersey, for life. I went through Lyndon Rive, the solicitor and, do you know, it was two years before he sent me a bill! About two guineas his fee was.

Although I'm now retired I am still entitled to write out prescriptions. There's a special list of drugs that dentists can prescribe and I have a copy and some prescription forms.

A la Cour Royale de l'Ile de Jersey.

L'An mil neuf cent QUARANTE-SIX, LE VINGT-QUATRIEME JOUR D'AOUT.

EX.

Sur la demande de Arthur Stanley Swain, Ecr., il lui est permis d'exercer la profession de Dentiste dans cette Ile et à l'appui de sa demande il a présenté un certificat émanant du "Dental Board of the United Kingdom" portant la date du 13e jour d'Août, 1946, et le seing de "D. Heidley Smith" Enregistreur, constantant qu'il est enregistré au Registre dit "Dentists Registe aux termes de l'Acte de Parlement intitulé "The Dentists Act, 1878" le tout en conformité de l'Article deux du Règlement passé par les Etats le 14 Mars, 1939, sur l'exercice de la profession de Dentiste dans cette Ile.

4

Permit to practise Dentistry.

I was five years in the dental practice at 26 Queen Street. Cyril Tanguy, he later became a States Deputy, was my landlord. He owned the building too. I paid somewhere around £75 a year or thirty shillings a week. I remember he also had the shop, a grocers, on the corner of Queen Street and Bath Street, where Dorothy Perkins is now. My surgery was over his shop. Bertha and Honorine De La Taste, the well known local florists, were in the flat above my surgery. Tanguys had the dairy on the corner opposite Royal Crescent as well.

We lived in several different flats at first and then we went out to La Rocque. We had a whole house there, which we shared with some friends, and Peggy's mother and father who came to live in the island. It was a big house, Rockview. Slap opposite the harbour itself it is, looks out to sea. We lived there for two years, and then we moved a bit further up the road to a house right on the opposite side, on a point, a rock really. Glenroyd they called it. We had sea on both sides of our bedroom. There wasn't a bathroom at Glenroyd, just the old tin bath you know and the toilet was fed by a cistern that collected rainwater from the roof, so if it ran dry you were in a bit of a pickle! We rented that house, thirty shillings a week, from Stanley England who was later to become Constable of Grouville. He bought it to retire to.

Ted Le Gresley was my solicitor then. He was very kind to me. It was when we had to leave Rockview that he said, "I know Glenroyd is vacant, go and see it. I think he might let you have it. There's someone in half the house but it's big and completely divided."

So I went to see Stanley England and he said, "Yes, you can have it."

My wife was expecting our first child, Michael, and I said, "How much would the rent be?"

I always get overcome when I remember his reply.

"What do you think you can afford?"

"Well," I said, "I can afford thirty shillings a week."

"Well, you can have it for that," he said.

You don't find people like that today.

Two of our children, Michael and Patricia, were born at Glenroyd. There was a good bus service in those days, along the coast road. Double-deckers we had then.

So I practiced from Queen Street for a few years then Joe Price, the dentist at the Hospital had a frightful stroke one January Monday morning. His receptionist at the Hospital, Miss May Croad, who was well known to a lot of islanders, rang me up at Glenroyd and asked me if I could possibly take the clinic that morning. She hadn't had time to cancel the patients. (I had done a clinic or two for him before, when he was on holidays, so she knew me.) Well I went down and did the clinic, and then we arranged another clinic later in the week. Gradually I got to do all the clinics, you see, because he never came back into dentistry. I did four or five mornings a week, and that was besides my own practice.

At the end of twelve months the Public Health Committee were

We too Remember When...

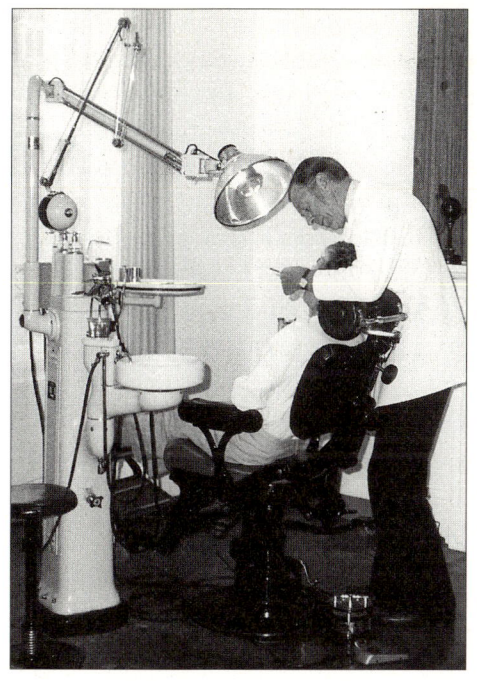

Arthur Swain at work.

required to advertise the job for a Dental Consultant, and naturally I applied and I think Edward Herivel applied as well. Anyway they gave me the job because I'd been doing it. That was in 1948. From then I did the consultancy job as well, which came finally to six mornings a week. It was hard work because with a dental practice your expenses are the same. You've a receptionist to pay for, rent to pay etc. and you're only there part time. A lot of the time you're working to pay off the expenses and it's only after that you get any profit for yourself. I got £450 a year from the Public Health which, though nothing compared to what is earned today, wasn't bad in those days. £9 a week, well, you know what men were earning in the late forties. It wasn't bad. Moreover, you had that the whole of the time, even when you were on holiday and of course it increased over the years.

When I started, the whole of the Hospital was the granite building, in Gloucester Street. The building still stands just as it did then but it's flanked left, right and centre by all the new places. The Dental Clinic was down the corridor to the left of the main door and foyer. The very end room it was. Two rooms. One was the surgery and the next was the recovery room. In the recovery room there was a row of hand basins with taps. The children had gas, as you know, and as soon as the tooth was out, before the child was back in this world, our strong porter would lift the child up, take it though the swing doors and pop it into the lap of its mother or sister. It was generally the women who brought the children.

We had a nurse, besides Miss Croad. So there'd be the Porter, Miss Croad, the anaesthetist giving the gas, a nurse and myself. In those days the anaesthetist was Dr Gardener on a Monday and his partner Dr Maitland, who was the official Hospital anaesthetist, took over on a Friday. Mr Halliwell was the only surgeon, assisted by a house surgeon.

There were fillings, though a lot would not have them. The thing was, you know, that sugar was de-rationed soon after I took the job on and the condition of the teeth of the children of this island absolutely plummeted. So I never used to fill milk teeth, but if I thought I could save the second teeth I used to say, when I was examining the mouths at the schools, "Filling... extraction... filling.... filling... extraction... extraction..."

But there weren't a great many takers for fillings. Things have changed a great deal, I mean, in those days most people only went to the dentist when their teeth ached, and they had their teeth out. When they'd got so few, or they'd got this disease that most people called Pyorrhoea, (that was partly due to the bad nourishment during the Occupation, and the poverty that followed afterwards) well, they'd have dentures. They just didn't get the vitamins.

You don't see it today, that disease. Chronic Supporative Perinontatis we used to call it. And as I said the sugar used to put paid to the milk teeth as well. Suddenly the shops were filled with sweets, and you could get all the sticky buns you wanted from the bakers. So it was a matter of a lot of extractions.

I went around the schools on Thursday mornings. There were twelve Parishes, but as there were more than twelve schools it meant that I saw more than one school a month. I did all the schools and, of course, in those days the schools were all ages. You went to your Parish school from the age of six until you left at fourteen. I saw all the country children, all the town schools too. All the States schools.

Harold Le Drouillenec, Headmaster of St. John's, used to organise a coach to bring the children down to have their teeth out. Their mothers could come as well. The coach would seat about forty. It was the same with Mr Anthony at St. Martin's. We used to have much better attendance from those schools because, of course, they were all kept together. I remember we've had as many as thirty children at one go, one after another. Fortunately I had a strong constitution. Not so much a right arm because it's a knack.

I remember a Centenier of Grouville whose children were down to go, "I don't believe in dentists!" he said.

As if it were Father Christmas!

And of course the Hospital job was a privilege as well because you saw all the things that the ordinary dentist didn't tackle like buried teeth, impacted wisdoms and cysts of the jaws (where the bone hollows out and a cyst forms inside.) I used to do those and, of course, fractured jaws.

Usually you'd get the call about one o'clock in the morning, when you're fast asleep. Usually something to do with drink. They were fighting, or someone walked into a lamp-post, or they'd a smash in the car. Then of course you've to wire the jaws up in the theatre. We've had as many as fourteen in a year, probably about one or so every month. It takes quite a long time and you've your own work to do the next day!

That was the interesting part of the job though, doing all the things a consultant dental surgeon has to do. And the thing was, you see, you couldn't send him down to that clever chap at the hospital down the road because you're here. You've got to do it, even if it's multiple fractures of the face. Perhaps twice, maybe three times in thirty-five years, I've had to send people over to London for very specialised work.

Before the imposition of the forty miles an hour speed limit there were some nasty smashes. People were tearing about at sixty and seventy miles an hour. Senator Troy, boss of the stevedores, he brought in the forty miles an hour speed limit. If he did nothing else he did a good thing there. He proposed it you know, saw it through.

The Dental Department is left very much to itself in most places, even on board ship. In the Navy, unlike the other Services, you're responsible to the Captain, not to the Senior Medical Officer. So the Dental Clinic was separate, within the Hospital, but any patients that'd had surgery and needed further medical attention went to the appropriate wards - mostly Male Surgical because, there again, you don't get many women with fractured jaws, unless they'd had an accident.

You see you've got to be gentle really because, when you think that most human flesh is 90% water, if you start pushing it about and I've seen people do this, pushing it about, it doesn't do. It doesn't heal as well. If you're gentle with the soft tissue you'll have better results.

I'm not a political animal so I never tried to delve into Hospital politics. There's always some people trying to enlarge their own little kingdom. We had a Matron in charge then, not the vast administration they have today. In those days we only had about three Civil Servants in the Hospital, now they seem to need assistants to the assistants! I remember, some years after the war, when the Hospital just topped half a million pounds to run for the year. That'd been the island's budget before the war! Yes, the whole island was run for half a million pounds. And then it came to the day when it cost that much just to run the Hospital. I remember that day. I can't tell you when it was, it may have been in the fifties or early sixties, something like that. Mind it costs millions now, just the Hospital. Shows how things have grown.

My David Place surgery? Incidentally I must tell you, it was Joe Price's (the original Hospital dentist's) place. The rental started at £90 a year and that was the whole house. The lower front room on the street was the waiting room, there was a small lounge behind that, a kitchen and a scullery. Then the room facing the street, directly above the waiting room, was the surgery and behind that, over the lounge, was the dental workshop where we made dentures and false teeth. Then there was a bathroom and separate toilet. On the next floor were two good sized bedrooms and above that were two attics, not bad attics actually. There was a very nice oak staircase with turned banisters all the way up and dado covered walls. There was a wooden ledge/handrail separating the lower part of the wall from the top which helped to keep the gloss painted paper clean. We only had a tiny yard at the back but it had an outside toilet. Our two children Michael and Patricia were quite happy playing down there.

At first I used to make the dentures in the evenings and Sunday mornings! Yes, I worked hard but we used to take Monday evenings off, Peggy and I. After that I used to have George Le Bouteloup, a local chap. He'd been trained as a dental mechanic when he was a young man. He used to work for Mr Parlett, who was the first qualified dental surgeon ever to practice in Jersey. Before that they were all unqualified. George had run a grocer's shop in the town for many years but he'd got a bit fed up and came and asked me for the job. He was very good with his hands but he was very lame with a T.B. hip. He worked for me for a long time, we got on very well. We used to do some good work. He died about five years ago.

My first receptionist was my wife Peggy, for almost three years, until we started a family. Peggy has a charming and easy way with people and this was a great asset in building up a practise. I didn't have a great succession of Dental Nurses to work for me because they stayed with me a long time. My next one, Joan Luce, was from a nice St. Clement family. They lived near the Church. She stayed with me until she got married. She married an Englishman and he took her over to England. They came back to Jersey and, as my receptionist had just left, Joan came back to work for me for a few more years before she left finally to start a family.

After a gap of about five years we had our third child, Caroline. She was a bit of a surprise. My wife had to run up two flights of stairs to the attics and it got a bit much. So we started to look around for another home. We bought our house in St. Clement but, naturally, we kept on the surgery. I'd had a word with the solicitor and he said we could do what we liked, so we sublet the flat. Rather stupidly, I suppose some people would think, I only charged a proportion of the rent. But then you see I never forgot what Stanley England had done for me and I wanted to pass it on. We had these good examples.

Greed begets greed. That's how it's all got out of hand today. People want everything today, car, television, fridge. We'd none of those at all when we were first married and we were as happy as anything. Peggy and I had been brought up in Sheffield, in not so affluent circumstances, without all the trappings so seemingly necessary today.

When I first came to Jersey there were twelve dentists in the island. Six of them qualified, six unqualified. The last unqualified dentist to practise was 'old Nolais', Mr Nolais in Don Street. He started off making dentures as a dental mechanic, as most of them did, and learned the profession as he went along. Three of the qualified – Edward Herivel, Bill Renouf and myself – were new from the Services. I was the first of the newcomers to start.

Generally speaking the farmers and growers wouldn't come to me unless they had the money. They paid on the dot. But there was a man, when we had the surgery in Queen Street, who used to come in on a Saturday afternoon. He had a complete upper denture and he used to say,

"Can I borrow ten bob on this please?"

And I lent it to him. It was for his Saturday night binge and ten bob was enough – well, it was probably enough for both Saturday and Sunday's drinking! In the middle of the week he'd come back with his ten bob and redeem his teeth. However, there came a time when I lent him the ten bob on his teeth and I never saw him again.

Visits to the Hospital when I was young were always filled with terror and the Dental Clinic was no exception. I can vividly remember the mental aberrations that I experienced before I lost consciousness, they followed the same pattern, and the mixed smell of rubber and chloroform only added to the panic which caused me to kick out against the nursing staff who held me down. It was always a relief to come to, head over the bowl, watching my red blood making a streaky pattern on the stark white porcelain. To know that I was safely back on one of my elder sister's knees and that, on either side of me, my friends would be in similar circumstances at each of the long line of basins.

Similarly my one and only stay in the children's ward left a deep impression. It was only a simple operation, the removal of a growth from my hand, but it meant staying in hospital for a week. The children's wards then were exactly the same as for the adults with no exceptions made in the way of decorations etc. but they were at the rear of the hospital, looking out onto the area of Kensington Place. We were not allowed to wear our own clothes and were given clean winceyette gowns each night and a clean gingham dress for the day.

I remember that it had its own operating theatre, a place we were terrified of being taken into because we could not help but see, hear and

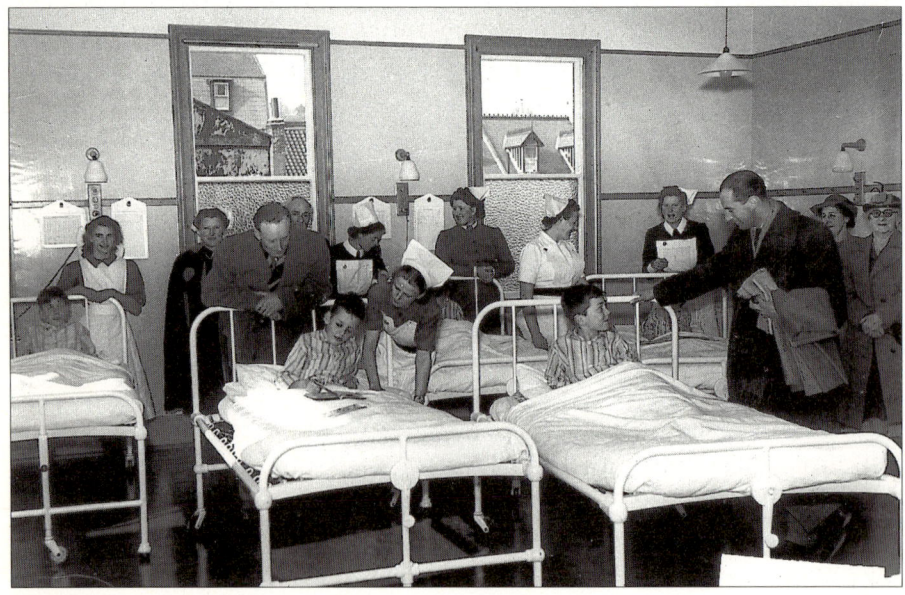

Children in the hospital ward, March 1949.
(Published by kind permission of *The Jersey Evening Post*).

witness the results of a visit to that room. The door leading to the theatre was on the side of the ward where the 'tonsils and adenoids' were put and we children on the other side watched as each of our friends, (three of my playmates were in for that operation at the time I was there) were brought out unconscious, heads hanging down, bloody mouths open, to avoid choking.

Though they were given the treat of 'ice-cream and jelly' for a few days afterwards I didn't envy them at all for they were not allowed visitors, in case of infection. Can you imagine how awful it must have been to have seen people crowd around the children on the other side of the ward, hear the conversations, see the presents? I remember asking my brother to take one of the comics that he'd brought me over to one of the boys who'd had a particularly sore throat.

All gifts of foodstuffs were taken away 'to be shared'. Quite willing to share with the other children in the ward, I remember looking forward to having half of one of the gorgeous fresh jam doughnuts, that my mother could ill have afforded but bought from Lockes, the baker in Saville Street, as a treat. But I never saw them again.

I remember too that once a day Sister would bring us each a sweet, just one, and on the day of my operation she put it on the windowsill for me to have later. Unfortunately it was too much of a temptation for one of the other children but I beat her to it, putting it in my mouth before she could grab it. Of course I was terribly sick!

Daff Noël

Madge Hayes, M.B.E., born 1911, remembers...

I was born in Belfast and trained to be a nurse at the Royal Victoria Hospital. My first job was in the nursery, then I worked in various departments before I moved to the Benn Hospital where I specialised in Ear, Nose and Throat.

I came to Jersey when I was nineteen, to work at the General Hospital, and was collected at the harbour in a horse and cart. It was 1930. The Ear, Nose and Throat ward, like most of the others, had about ten beds and we worked directly under Mr Ratazzi. During the time I was at the hospital the consultants and doctors always waited on us junior staff at the Christmas Dinner. It was a lovely practice. I had some very good times at the Hospital. As young nurses we would walk down to the beach at West Park for a quick dip during our break, and do our studying up amongst the trees of Westmount.

Hospital staff, 1933. Madge is fifth from the right in the top row and Dr. Ratazzi is fourth from the right in the front.

Then one day I accidentally pushed a young man, Herbert (Bert) Beuzeval, down the stairs – so I married him! I have three sons – Bertie, Phillip and David and five grandchildren... I think! Bertie is retired and Phillip is a Methodist Minister with a big church in Oxford. David is the only one who has stayed over here. They're good boys. If I had a dozen I'd want them to be all boys. They were all born at the Maternity Hospital, which is now the Le Bas Centre, in St. Saviour's Road.

During the war we evacuated to Newport, South Wales where I worked with the local people who needed help. After my husband died in 1958 I became Mrs Timothy Hayes but was widowed again in 1979. I was the first lady to be elected to the St. Helier Community Services Board. I enjoyed that, the same as I enjoyed being President of the Soroptomist Club of Jersey. I've always enjoyed being involved with people.

We too Remember When...

> **Eileen Barette née Amy** *was born at Mont Mado Stores in 1928, when Mont Mado was a real little village...*

It still is a real little village but our shop's not there any more. That was turned into a private house some time ago.

My grandparents moved there in 1905, when my grandmother was three months pregnant with my mum. T.B. was rampant in the family when my grandmother died there later, at the age of forty-five. My mother automatically took the shop over.

It was, what I call, a real old-fashioned shop. There were hooks in the ceiling where you hung up the scrubbing brushes, the buckets, the Wellington boots, and an old paraffin lamp. We sold red handkerchiefs, stockings, pinafores, sewing cotton, needles and darning wool. At the back of the shop, there must have been between twenty-five or thirty little drawers full of different sized nails, shoe-laces and little things like that. There were even the iron heel and toe tips for the clogs and shoes from my grandmother's time!

We also sold corn for the chickens. Flour and sugar came in one hundred pound hessian bags – the bags were later washed and made into aprons! We had to weigh out the flour and sugar with a scoop into three pound bags, that was your job when it rained, and afterwards you always put the bags on top of the crates of cherryade.

When I was a little girl we were the off-licence of the island who sold the most beer. That was because of Mont Mado Quarries. Oh! I was brought up with the workers drinking in the back shed: they'd come in, go down to the shed at the bottom of the shop, picking up three bottles on the way, and they'd say,

"Two beers, one stout!"

And my mother used to put it in the book. Then on a Friday, when they were paid, they'd pay their bill for the week and start again.

The shed was at the bottom of the shop, through a door. The copper was housed down there and bags of coal, and wood to light the range. There was a clothes-horse too, because in those days when you washed your clothes you put them on the horse when the weather was bad. There was a wooden tub and in the corner was a five hundred gallon drum of paraffin. We used to fill people's cans from it.

Talk about safety today being over the top! Those men would go down to that end of the shop – well imagine, there were these men, all smoking pipes, sittings on logs and drinking their beer. Drinking two or three bottles every night, of a lunch time and every Friday 'til eight o'clock... and five hundred gallons of paraffin in the corner!! Yeh!

When I was growing up in the village ninety per cent of the men worked at the quarry, as stonemasons, things like that. They had pretty large families – four, six, or more children, and when the winter was hard... I mean you can't work with stone if the weather freezes because the stone cracks. In those days if you didn't work, you didn't get paid.

My parents used to carry them but talk about the honest poor! I've always heard of one family that couldn't pay my parents for seven weeks. But what could you do? You couldn't let six children starve!

But then the village was really one big family, everybody knew everybody else. You walked into each other's home... Absolute! If they were eating bread and butter and you wanted one, well, you had one made for you as well... Oh yes. So my mother always said to the quarry workers' families,

"Don't worry, when the days are longer in the summer, and it's fine, you'll be able to repay me."

And this one family – do you know the man left his job at the quarry and did the potato season, because he knew he'd be better paid and able to pay my mother back sooner? Yeh! People were more honest then. No H.P., eh!

My father was a carpenter by trade and worked for Boniface from St. Aubin's before the war. He'd go off on his motor bike at seven o'clock in the morning and come back at six o'clock at night and, I was the eldest, the first thing he'd do when he'd taken his coat off was give me a rider-a-doh around the table. Now a rider-a-doh is when you climb on their back and have a ride. That was my treat of the evening! Afterwards he'd have his dinner and then he'd start work by going into that bottom shed where the men had been drinking and sorting all the empty bottles, so that when the brewery came it was all done for them. After that he'd go to his workshop and file saws till around nine p.m.

Obviously when the Germans came there was no work at Bonifaces so he was put down and he came back to work in the shop.

Now nobody had thought to look through those little drawers at the back of the shop but come the Occupation (and Eileen was as hard as she is now on her shoes – I could eat the leather like I eat bread and butter!), those iron tips came out of that drawer and taken with my shoes to the cobbler. The cobbler was also the caretaker of St. John's School

We too Remember When...

and our school corridors were tiled, so can you imagine Eileen! We had a Miss Phoebe Bisson, an old spinster, a very, very stern, but good, teacher and she'd shout,

"Eile-e-n! Can't you walk quietly?"

And of course, the more you were told not to, the more you did! But no, I was never punished at school, well, not the cane. A few lines yes, but otherwise I was quite good. When I first started at St. John's there were only four classes, then in 1935/6 they built a new Infants' Class, as they called it, that was a lovely big class. Glass all around with a big veranda.

The boys and girls were always separated. Oh! Yes! There was an 8-10 feet high wall across the playground! The girls went in one entrance and the boys went in another... And when you were sitting in class the girls were in the front and the boys were in the back! Oh, yes. You weren't mixed at all.

There were about twenty-two children in the little classes but when you got to the top class, as we called it, there was a lot more. We were six in a row of desks and about five or six rows deep. That was Mr Journeaux's class. The Headmaster took his own class in those days. Our desks were box-like with the lid and of course an inkwell, in a big room with a fireplace at both ends. I was at St. John's all my school life.

Yes, the village school was nice. Very, very nice. The Headmaster, as I said, was Bert Journeaux. He was a marvellous man. My school days were really, really lovely.

And another thing about school then – you banked your money once a week. The schools collected it for the Penny Savings Bank. Every Monday morning you took your penny, tuppence, thruppence, or sometimes you had a sixpence, and when you had saved a pound you took your bank book to school with you and the teacher transferred the pound from your little card into your bank book. Every year the Rector used to come and give sixpence to each girl and boy that had banked every Monday of the year. So that was quite a thing if you never missed, eh. Oh! and you had thruppence if you never missed school, and thruppence if you were the best needle-woman! It taught us to save, for even if you only had a penny you were rewarded for saving it. Reverend Nicolle was the Rector of St. John then. I can still see him, a doddery old man.

When I was going to school there'd be ten or twelve kids going to school at the same time, all walking of course. Never anything else. There might be a car in the garage, a bike in the shed, but you had two legs and you used them. Rain, hail, sunshine or snow, we walked four times a day. There was a bus stop outside the shop but you didn't jump on. We never got bored, because if you'd mentioned the word you'd have been given a duster or a brush and mother would have found something for you to do, that's for sure!

My parents worked very hard and they saved. My mother never spent a penny if she could save a halfpenny. There were sweets in the shop but we were never allowed to take one. You never went to a jar to take a sweet unless you had asked and been told you could. They retired in 1966. The shop wasn't their property.

I remember when I was a little girl, in the early thirties, my father wanted to buy the property, it belonged to Jurat Hocquard at the time. The Jurat had a son who was going to inherit so my father didn't have the opportunity to buy it. Of course when Jurat Hocquard died his son didn't want it, by which time my parents were much older and they had bought the next lot of cottages that were attached to the shop.

They were just cottages, you know, just the downstairs, eh. Just one floor, two tenants. One tenant was a good payer and the other one wasn't, so he was made to move out. Then the tenant that was the good payer moved into that cottage and my parents built up the other. When it was ready the good tenants moved back in. Do you know the daughter of the tenant moved out last October? She had lived seventy years there!

My father died in 1992, my mother in 1995, and do you know when my sister and I were sorting out my mother's things we found all her ledgers from the shop, from when the customers charged their groceries and paid once a week. Sugar, flour, candles, paraffin! Well, sometime later my grandaughter was doing a project for school and my daughter asked if she could have a look at these books. The girl was studying them and suddenly she said to my daughter,

"Mum, do you know what they haven't got in these books?"

My daughter said no.

"There's no toilet paper!"

But of course there wasn't! Her mother explained how we used to tear the *Morning News* or *Evening Post* into four, push a nail through a corner, thread through a piece of string, and hang it on a nail in the lavatory. You couldn't do that now with the way the print comes off!

I was taught to darn. We had a treadle sewing machine and I used to mend all my own, my sister's and my father's clothes. I knew how to turn collars and cuffs, replace pockets, patch trousers, and turn the outside of sheets to the middle.

I married from the shop and moved just up the road, into one of my Dad's houses at Eileenid Villas – the middle one. I had a scullery, a nice sized dining room with a range, and a big lounge with a tiled fireplace. A lovely staircase took you up to the two big double bedrooms and then on to two singles. There were lovely bay windows at the front of the house and a lavatory up the garden, no bathroom in those days of course. We lived there for six years before moving here.

I've been at Malta House since November 1949. When Roy and I moved in I was seven months pregnant with my youngest daughter Gwen and do you know when my parents retired they went to live in the house I moved into when I first married!

Did I know my husband Roy all my life? No, but both families did! My father-in-law and my mum went to school together. My father-in-law lived at Thornhill, which is just across the field, and their first two babies were born there, my husband and a brother. My father-in-law was J.H. Barette, the merchant, and when my mother-in-law was pregnant with her third one – 'cos you didn't have cars in those days – they decided they'd move to a house they'd bought, Altona, in St. Mark's Road. They thought it would be easier for my father-in-law to come and go, and for the children to go to school, things like that.

Then comes the threat of war – child number seven had arrived – and my father-in-law thought it was too dangerous to live in the town. So he decided to rent a house out in the country, at the back of St. Martin's Public Hall, called Carteret. He bought the boys a bike for going to school (they went to the Beeches) but the news was getting worse and worse. There was the big decision about whether to evacuate or not, and with seven children they decided 'yes'. Of course, with my father-in-law being in business he knew lots of business people in England and knew just where he was going. So he dumped everything in the car, the kids and what they could carry, but before going to the pier he said,

"We'll just pop into Altona and listen to the news for the last time."

Well, they listened to the news and found that where they were going had been bombed. So he turned to my mother-in-law and said,

"If we're going to die we might as well die in Jersey!"

The car was turned around and they all went back to St. Martin's! Obviously they scratched their heads and wondered what they were going to do, and thought about this house. Now Malta House has been in the family since it was built for grandfather, Captain Joseph Barette. He was

Daff Noël

a Captain of schooners and had named the house after Malta, because of the many times he had sailed into there.

Now at the time of the war the house was let to a young couple who had been married three years (Mr and Mrs De Caux who used to own the Belle Étoile). This was their first home), and my father-in-law came to see them and an arrangement was made to halve it. So the young couple moved to the end of the house where they had a kitchen, a scullery, a dining room and the good bedroom above.

The Barettes, being ten of them, needed the remainder. (Even then the children didn't have their own room, no way. There were three boys to a small room, the maid – they always had a maid – had two children in with her, Betty, the only girl, was in the box room, and then mum and dad and the baby in the main room.)

They also had the dining room-cum-sitting room and their kitchen. They had a big table in their kitchen and, oh, it was just like Snow White and the Seven Dwarfs. All the bowls were different sizes! Seven kids with the eldest having the biggest bowl, the next a smaller one, and so on all around the table! Dad sat at the top and Mum sat the other side with the maid.

I went in one day to find Roy with a pinny on. All the children had one, each with their name on. It was an all-in-one, over your head. They never sat at table without their pinny. O-Oh! No!

The maid ate with them. She has always been regarded as one of the family. She was there when the sixth baby was born and you can say she brought him up. If you came here any evening about half past four you'd find her on the step with her enamel dish and the big urn with water in, doing her spuds for tomorrow. Half past four, always. Then after tea all the shoes were brought to the step and she cleaned them for the morning, before putting them in a row under the children's coats.

I met Roy when he came to live here, the shop being just up the road, also my mum and his aunt knew each other very, very well. On that first Saturday evening Aunty Dor, as we called her, came to the shop to see if I would wait for Betty the following morning to walk with her to Chapel – you went to chapel in those days – Les Frères we went to.

I can remember that first Sunday... there was my sister and I, all changed with our hats on... you know, waiting... and there were these four boys, all in their Beeches uniform, caps and all, walking up the hill, with Betty. We all walked to Chapel together, so of course we all got to be very friendly. I was less than twelve, yes, less than twelve when I met my husband. We were always good friends from when we used to play hide and seek and all that.

He never had another girl and I never had another boy. In those days the Beeches had Thursday afternoons off and went in on Saturdays for the morning. So on the Thursday he used to come and meet me from school, on his bike.

As I said I got married from the shop in 1944. I was sixteen. What was my wedding like? Oh! God, my wedding was like nobody else's wedding! My husband and all his brothers cycled to St. Saviour's Church but I was allowed a taxi. We came back in it, then the next day they went to fetch the bikes. We came here, to Malta House and the reception, if you want to call it that. Just the family. Mind you there was seven children already in my in-laws' family and mum and dad and the maid, well that was ten. Then there were Roy's two first cousins, my sister and I, and my mum and dad. That's all that we were. But at a quarter to ten in the evening you had to leave to get home before curfew!

My father had built three houses, you see, and it was a stroke of luck that the middle one was empty so we were able to move in. But next morning, at seven o'clock Roy was up and back here to milk the cows. You don't get time off on farms you know! The Barettes were merchants, and all the other boys were in the business, but the grandparents ran the farm. Roy was the only one who wanted to farm.

Roy was a Centenier for eleven years. He had been the youngest C.O. in the island, twenty-one, then from C.O. he went to Vingtenier, which he hated. For in those days the Vingtenier collected the rates. You didn't go to the Parish Hall then. The Vingtenier's home was open for people to pay their rates. Oh! yes, he had the Rate Book at home and people would come here. So you would have all that money at home. Roy didn't like anything to do with money. It was always me who dealt with that.

Then they were looking around for a Centenier. He came back one day and he said,

"You know Eileen I'm going to be asked to be...."

"No way!" I said. "You're not going to be a Centenier – No way are you going to be the servant of people! Who's going to be left to do all the work on the farm? Me? No way!"

He told me that if it was up to him he would enjoy the work. So anyway, there was one more man that they still had to ask and they made arrangements that they'd go up to see him that evening.

Before Roy left he said, "You know, if he turns it down it's going to be me next." Huh! I thought.

Well, in those days you bathed in the tin bath in front of the fire and I remember I'd had my bath, and was in my clean pyjamas, when he came back, like a little dog with his tail between his legs! As we were going upstairs he said, "Edgar Simon is coming to see you tomorrow morning."

Ah well, neither of us slept well that night. We didn't discuss it but we knew it was a decision we had to make. And the next morning Edgar Simon and the old man, Phil Romeril, came. Edgar said, "You know what we've come for...?"

And I said, "Yes, and I don't want Roy to be Centenier. No way!"

Well, we all talked, and talked, and probably about an hour, hour and a half later, I said to Roy, "Well, if you really want the job..."

But I must say, after all that, I thoroughly enjoyed it. Absolutely! Thoroughly enjoyed it! I put my heart into it, like Roy. I didn't know everything that was going on, because you know what goes on behind closed doors is not to be repeated, but some things you have to know because if the police phone....

We'd been married twenty-seven years when he died. This young couple came to see me and, as they were leaving, she turned round to me and said, "It was your husband who saved our marriage."

I looked at her.

"You didn't know?" she said, "Yes, we went through a very rocky patch and he came not once, but two or three times, and he'd sit and he'd chat, and he saved our marriage."

He was that sort of bloke who had all the time in the world for people.

We had a very happy marriage, give and take, no secrets from one another, and good friends. And we had been very young when we'd got married. Everybody said it wouldn't last long but we showed them.

He hated rows. In our twenty-seven years of marriage there's been only three big rows, what I call big, with tempers that are really at the very top of the ladder, and when it got like that he spoke so quick and so fumbled that you didn't have a clue what he'd said! He'd bang on the table and bellow, and then he'd walk out.

He'd walk to the gate, turn back, and it would be 'my love...' All forgotten! He'd had his say and that was it, and it would never, ever, be brought up again. He never held grudges.

I can remember one, and that wasn't long after we were here... it was after the planting season and Roy'd probably gone on a police case... I'd

We too Remember When...

Eileen and Roy

told the Frenchman, "There's the empty potato boxes in the field, you can go and fetch them and bring them in."

Well, he came back and said they were gone.

"Gone? Can't be!" I said.

"Oui, Oui, Madame Barette, c'est vrai!"

When Roy came back he said he'd told his brother he could help himself. I was furious – after all, I worked on the farm as well – and for him to do this without telling me! I was so mad, I cried!

That afternoon I went to town and when I returned he said, "We're going to the pictures tonight." A real treat. When we got back there was this huge bouquet of flowers on the doorstep.

He'd phoned up Arthur Jouanny who, at the time, lived up the lane and had a place in the market, told him he was taking me to the pictures and wanted the flowers delivered while we were out. Arthur asked what sort of card did he want?

"Just a forgiving one!" Roy said.

That's the sort of man he was. But then all his family are like that. Good as gold.

We gave up the farm in 1965.

~

The Agricultural Shows at Springfield were always very dressed up affairs. The men had nice suits on, with ties, and the women all dressed up in their very best attire. I can remember being petrified of cows and having to walk amongst them afterwards, and always trying to think up a reason to escape somehow! I only went for the socialising, because afterwards we'd have a tea dance at the Pavilion.

In the winter, particularly when they had the Drag Hunt, we would follow the Hunt, after that a tea dance at the Pavilion, then go on to the first house pictures which came out at nine o'clock, then back to each other's home for supper! There were about eight of us in my little group of friends so that meant that one Thursday night in eight you would be host. All our boyfriends were mostly working in banks so Thursday was their afternoon off. Did I ride with the Hunt? Oh! Good gracious no, I'm terrified of horses! No, I followed in my car. It was quite a social event.

Then, of course, I think in those days people dressed properly, didn't they? Not like today when you don't see people dress up, even at big functions. It's such a shame.

Kay Wills

I liked the way we used to go down to the boat and greet or wave goodbye to people. It's so impersonal now. We often go to the Scillies and it's just like being transported back to what our harbour was like years ago.

Reverend Geoffrey Baker

On summer Saturday nights we used to go and spend a couple of hours down the harbour. We met the same people every week. We used to congregate down the end of the Albert Pier and watch the mail boats coming in and going out. In the season there'd be three or four potato boats going out. It'd be nothing to see six or seven potato boats being loaded up at the same time. We had two mail boats every day and on Saturdays we used to have two in the morning and usually two again in the evening. We had the *St. Helier* and the *St. Julien* on the Great Western side and the *Isle of Jersey, Isle of Sark* and the *Isle of Guernsey* on the southern side and they were all running in the summer. All five boats used to come in on the Saturday. Mind you, they weren't all that comfortable to travel on.

I've always been keen on boats and still am. I'll buy any book on Jersey shipping as soon as it comes out! I'll often walk around the harbour. We used to do that as kids you see, from about seven or eight. We were only allowed along the top walks of the Albert Pier though. We used to spend all our summer holidays either there or on West Park beach. That's changed face too of course, West Park, with its new slip and the way the Castle is now hidden from one's approaching view.

Pat Letto

We too Remember When...

Whenever I came home to Jersey it was always via the Harbour and my dad was always there to meet me. It was always a lovely homecoming. You'd see people on the pier-head as the boat came around the Castle and you'd wave to them. It was the same when you went to meet anyone. You could go right down to the end of the pier. You can't do that now.

Kay Wills

Irene Hurley née Maiden, born in 1946, remembers...

Growing up as a teenager in the late 50's and 60's in Jersey was great fun. Jersey, like England, was exciting and vibrant. Elvis Presley and his contemporaries had just started to change the face of music, and entertainment in general was 'in'. My generation, in my opinion, were very lucky to be there, right at the start!

The Opera House was still a cinema when 'Jail House Rock' was first screened, although no-one called it the Opera House then. The locals had given it the somewhat dubious title of 'the flea-pit'. This I think was slightly unfair and was probably more to do with the fact that it was one of the smallest and oldest of the six cinemas then flourishing in the island, than its general cleanliness.

In those days we had the Odeon Cinema, one large theatre on two floors and the Forum Cinema in Grenville Street which were on a par in size. But I always remember that large organ at the Forum complete with a male organist on a stool rising up majestically in front of the screen before each performance, entertaining us until the programme began. The New Era cinema at Georgetown, the tiny cinema at Gorey and last but not least we had a small cinema at Wests Centre. I'll never forget queuing at the Wests Cinema to see 'Psycho', it was rated an X-Certificate but we all thought we looked old enough (16) to get in. The manager however, a Mr Mitchell, had different ideas. He knew me well because I had a Saturday job in the cake shop across the road and when our group reached the front he let all my friends in and sent me home! The humiliation of it left me harbouring serious intentions of poisoning his next Saturday purchase!

Above the Wests Cinema was the Plaza Ballroom, where summer shows were put on for the visitors and during the winter all sorts of 'dos' were staged – from children's parties to celebrity shows. One of the most memorable for me was when Billy Fury was in concert there – 'Halfway To Paradise' was in the Top 20 at the time and he was one of my idols.

Springfield Stadium was used for many things apart from sport. Trade Fairs and Ideal Home Exhibitions were two, but the roller skating rink, which took over the entire floor area, was an absolute must on a weekend. I kept my white calf-height boots for years – my own children even learned to skate with them! My aunt made us (my sister and I) short skating skirts and, in groups, we were taught the steps for barn dancing and several others, the names of which escape me. But the euphoria of sweeping round those corners backwards at high speed, skates crossing one behind the other, still makes me tingle when I think of it. It was also at Springfield that I first saw a relatively unknown group called 'The Beatles'. The overpowering recollection I have of them, apart from the music of course, was the fact that they wore Beatle jackets and white shoes.

Lots of stars came to the island back then. Of course there were plenty of venues and plenty of visitors to fill them. The Sunshine Hotel, Swansons, the Wests Plaza, the Watersplash & the Strip, Tams, the Ritz Ballroom and the West Park Pavilion – then later came Caesar's Palace, the New Med, the Chateau Plaisir and the Belle Étoile. These were just a few of the places to choose from.

Many hotels staged their own in-house shows, either on a small scale or by enlisting acts from shows at other venues. When some stars had finished their stint at one venue they would drive to another and perform for a second time in one night. Places like Pontins and the Jersey Holiday Camp quite often used this method of entertaining their guests.

Apart from Billy Fury and the Beatles, I remember seeing Michael Holiday, Gerry Dawsey (now Englebert Humperdinck), Frankie Howard and Marti Caine, to name but a few.

The Strip, on the Five Mile Road, was particularly popular as a night club with a resident group fronted by Buddy Britton, who sang 'Zippity Doo Dah', and who is now an established author under his own name of Simon Raverne.

The Rainbow Room, which was over the New Era Cinema, was another extremely popular nightspot. Everybody, but everybody, went there. The live group playing there at the time was called 'The Crescendos' and they were fronted by a guy called George.

As time went on laws on drinking and driving became much stricter and this took its toll, together with waning visitor numbers on out of

We too Remember When...

town venues, thus heralding the demise of most of the cabarets.

They say you only remember the good things, and they're probably right because I remember long, hot, balmy summers, pubs full of sun-burnt happy visitors – that holiday island feeling which I fear will never return. Yes, people did drink and drive but I don't recall there being lots of horrific accidents yet, there again, there were a lot less cars on the roads I suppose, and statistics confirm that the weather was no better then than it is now. Even so, I still remember my youth as a great time and wouldn't swop with today's teenagers for anything.

Our mongrel dog, Prince, used to lie in the middle of the road in Mont Cochon. He used to wander off, living his own secret little life then come back a few days later, resume his place in the road in front of our gate, only moving leisurely to one side when a car honked its horn.

It was sunshine, not shadow, in those days. Our life was simple, we didn't expect too much. We were happy and contented. We weren't afraid. Not like nowadays.

Now some of us dread tomorrow. We look over our shoulder if we hear someone coming up too close to us.

We enjoyed our childhood. We were children in an adult world and we respected our elders. They only had to shout "Oi!" and we ran like hell. Not now. Now you get a mouthful of cheek.

Jill De Sousa

I don't think the world today is as good as in my youth because we used to make our own amusements. Our friendships were simpler but wholesome. Relationships have changed.

Alicia Priddy

We were fortunate in one respect in that we never saw how the rich lived but by experiencing the hard times, growing up in the Jersey of years ago, you appreciate all you have achieved since. Unfortunately a lot of youngsters today take it all for granted.

Constable Bob Le Brocq

For years after the end of the Occupation, the industries of the island were working on the land, growing and dairy farming, and tourism, traditional occupations. These days of course the main revenue is the Finance Industry, which is nothing to do with Jersey life, but exists because of international monetary laws. This has altered the whole character of life in Jersey.

Arthur Swain

*The following pages feature books
published by Seaflower Books
on Jersey and the Channel Islands.*

All these books may be obtained through your local bookshop or direct from the publisher, post-free on receipt of net price, at the following address:

1 The Shambles
Bradford on Avon
Wiltshire
BA15 1JS

Tel/Fax 01225 863595

Please enclose cheque or quote
Access/Visa/Amex credit or debit card number.

SEAFLOWER BOOKS on Jersey

JERSEY ALPHABET
by John Le Dain
An A to Z of over one hundred topics which have their basis in Island history and culture. The Occupation and the more obvious tourist attractions have been omitted; rather you will discover an entertaining and enlightening account of many aspects of Jersey life, both present day and in the past.
128 pages; Illustrated; ISBN 0 948578 84 X; Price £4.95

JERSEY IN LONDON
A History of the Jersey Society in London, 1896-1989
by Brian Ahier Read
This book tells the story of how, in late Victorian London, a small group of Jersey expatriates grew into a flourishing organisation. Its members have included some of the most eminent Jersey people of the century; it played a key role in helping refugees in 1940 when 30,000 people evacuated from the Channel Islands.
'An enthralling account.'
192 pages; Illustrated; ISBN 0 948578 64 5; Price £6.95

THE JERSEY LILY
The Life and Times of Lillie Langtry
by Sonia Hillsdon
Born Emilie Le Breton in Jersey in 1853, married to Edward Langtry at the age of twenty, Lillie Langtry was destined to be universally known an 'The Jersey Lily', the most beautiful woman in the world. Sonia Hillsdon's faithful account of Lillie's life and times makes enthralling reading.
128 pages; Illustrated; ISBN 0 948578 63 7; Price £4.95

JERSEY: NOT QUITE BRITISH:
The Rural History of a Singular People
by David Le Feuvre
The author outlines the events which have helped to form the special character of the men and women who were Jersey's original inhabitants ... 'This is gripping reading, colourful, proud and sad. It is not only an enlightening and entertaining work, but also an important one, whose author has done Jersey an enduring service by vividly conveying and recording the true nature of what is lost.'
160 pages; Illustrated; ISBN 0 948578 57 2; Price £5.95

JERSEY OCCUPATION DIARY
Her Story of the German Occupation, 1940-45
by Nan Le Ruez
This remarkable book is based on a diary which the author added to daily throughout the five long years of the Occupation. It is a deeply personal account and a uniquely authentic record, written from day to day, without hindsight and with no thought of eventual publication.
304 pages; Illustrated; ISBN 0 948578 61 0; Price £9.95

JERSEY RAMBLES: *Coast and Country*
by John Le Dain
If you wish to experience Jersey beyond its car parks, beaches and more obvious tourist attractions, this book will take you there. Enthusiastic and well informed, *Jersey Rambles* is the essential companion to walking the Island's footpaths.
128 pages; Illustrated; ISBN 0 948578 37 8; Price £4.95

JERSEY WEATHER AND TIDES
by Peter Manton
This book presents the essence of a lifetime's interest and accumulated wisdom.
96 pages; Illustrated; ISBN 0 948578 75 0; Price £5.95

THE MOTOR CAR IN JERSEY
by David Scott Warren
Just about every aspect of Jersey's century-long association with the motor car is included here. The author's text is informed by considerable knowledge of the subject as well as by an unmistakable enthusiasm, and is supported by an interesting and wide-ranging collection of pictures.
128 pages; Illustrated; ISBN 0 948578 68 8; Price £6.95

WANDERUNGEN UND STREIFZUGE AUF JERSEY
German language edition of **JERSEY RAMBLES** – see above
ISBN 0 948578 91 2; Price £5.95

WILD ISLAND: *Jersey Nature Diary*
Words by Peter Double; Pictures by Nick Parlett
'The combination of Peter Double's extensive knowledge of Jersey's natural life and his friendly, entertaining writing and Nick Parlett's delightful drawings make this diary a delight both for nature lovers and those who enjoy fine art.'
120 pages; Illustrated; ISBN 0 948578 77 7; Price £7.95

SEAFLOWER BOOKS on the Channel Islands in general

NO CAUSE FOR PANIC
Channel Islands Refugees, 1940-45
by Brian Ahier Read
'This interesting and important book fills a significant gap in the history of the Channel Islands during the Second World War. Packed with fascinating detail culled from diaries and memoirs, it describes the evacuation experiences, beginning with the journeys of those Channel Islanders, many of them children, some of them babies, who left the Islands for war-time Britain in 1940.'
160 pages; Illustrated; ISBN 0 948578 69 6; Price £6.95

THE SEA WAS THEIR FORTUNE
A Maritime History of the Channel Islands
by Roy McLoughlin
'McLoughlin has done a remarkable job of pulling together the strands of the islands' history, often working with the sketchiest of sources to produce a book which is highly readable and entertaining.'
160 pages; Illustrated; ISBN 0 948578 86 6; Price £5.95

SEAFLOWER BOOKS on Guernsey and Sark

GUERNSEY COUNTRY DIARY:
Through the Natural Year with Nigel Jee
This book is one man's record of the world of nature in the Channel Island of Guernsey. Nigel Jee, known to readers of the *Guernsey Evening Press* for his regular 'Country Column', brings a lifelong fascination with all aspects of the natural world to bear on his observations and cogitations. Justine Peek is a young Guernsey artist whose specially prepared illustrations beautifully complement the author's account.
128 pages; Illustrated; ISBN 0 948578; Price £4.95

LIFE ON SARK by Jennifer Cochrane
Copiously illustrated with a selection of the author's own photographs and drawings, this well informed and fondly written book is guaranteed to delight anyone intrigued by this island gem.
128 pages; Illustrated; ISBN 0 948578 63 7; Price £4.95